The Family Garden

Clever Things to Do In, Around &
Under the Garden

JAN & MICHAEL GERTLEY

Sterling Publishing Co., Inc.
New York

Written, Illustrated and Photographed by Jan and Michael Gertley
Edited by Claire Bazinet
Designed by Judy Morgan

Library of Congress Cataloging-in-Publication Data
Gertley, Jan.
The family garden : clever things to do in, around & under
the garden / Jan and Michael Gertley.
p.   cm.
Includes index.
ISBN 0-8069-6154-6
1. Gardening. 2. Garden ornaments and furniture.
3. Nature craft. I. Gertley, Michael. II. Title.
SB453.G39   1997
635—dc21   97-15278
CIP

2   4   6   8   10   9   7   5   3   1

Published by Sterling Publishing Company, Inc.
387 Park Avenue South, New York, N.Y. 10016
© 1997 by Jan and Michael Gertley
Distributed in Canada by Sterling Publishing
%Canadian Manda Group, One Atlantic Avenue, Suite 105
Toronto, Ontario, Canada M6K 3E7
Distributed in Great Britain and Europe by Cassell PLC
Wellington House, 125 Strand, London WC2R 0BB, England
Distributed in Australia by Capricorn Link (Australia) Pty Ltd.
P.O. Box 6651, Baulkham Hills, Business Centre, NSW 2153, Australia
Printed in China
All rights reserved

Sterling ISBN 0-8069-6154-6

To our parents...
Whose love and nurturing
produced two little sprouts with skyward dispositions!

ACKNOWLEDGMENTS

We are grateful to the Johnson family for their friendship and generous participation in this project; a special family that added smiles, animation and love to our photographs. Thank you!

Our thanks also extend to Rebekah for joining us at our tea party and to Calvin and Sheana for adding their creative touches to the gourd birdhouses.

We also want to acknowledge our neighbors for their friendship and support: Rud and BJ for their laughs and pizza, and Sharon, Cheryl and Katrina for bringing in our hay during a very busy summer.

Contents

Introduction

A tiny Tudor cottage, just big enough for a child, stood in our backyard. We called it the bean house. Like a fairy tale cottage, twining bean vines embraced its walls and the wee front door welcomed only the smallest of visitors. The front path was flanked with a profusion of flowers that greeted the guests as they arrived. On sunny summer days the cottage was alive with activity. We would often see small green frogs swaying in the breeze as they rode on the upturned flower heads. Lumbering bumblebees would sound their familiar low buzz as they bounced from petal to petal. By far, however, the most active visitors that came to the bean house were children.

Children were delighted by the cottage. They loved playing in it and, in August, they enjoyed harvesting the beans. Giggles would come from inside the house: "We're picking beans from the ceiling!"

The popularity of the bean house inspired us to design an entire family garden. A garden in which a child's imagination is turned loose, exploration is encouraged, and learning is always fun. The bean house was just the beginning! What child wouldn't love to see dolphins frolicking off the bow of a boat "floating" in a sea of deep-blue lobelia? Or learn to tell the time from a seven-foot sundial? Or harvest vegetables from a horse-drawn wagon? It's all possible in the Family Garden.

Beasley guarding the front door of our original bean house

This book is a collection of garden projects that involve the whole family. The projects come together smoothly with easy-to-follow, step-by-step instructions. Once they are assembled, you may choose to follow the painting guidelines provided or decorate the projects using your own imagination. The gardening tips and techniques will help to ensure a successful gardening experience for everyone. By summer's end, your garden will be bursting with produce. Children can choose from a variety of projects and recipes that teach them how to use their harvest in new and perhaps surprising ways. Whether you create the entire garden, or just one or two projects, your whole family will enjoy gardening and learning together.

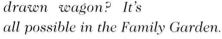

Part One

An Overview

An overview of the garden in early summer

The bean house was the first garden project we designed for children. As we developed the idea, we were guided by our memories of childhood. We remembered building forts and hideaways with small doors that made it difficult for adults to enter; we liked our toys to be scaled-down versions of the real thing; and we loved to play in the dirt and "help" mom and dad in the garden.

These memories not only inspired the bean house, but also many aspects of the other family garden props and projects. But, to design a garden the whole family would enjoy, we also drew inspiration from our passions as adults. We love to garden. We enjoy spending time in our outdoor living spaces, so they have to be inviting, aesthetically pleasing, neat and tidy, and functional. By combining the criteria set forth by both our adult and childhood desires, we designed the layout and props for the Family Garden.

The overall dimensions of the garden (32' × 32') allowed plenty of room to play, garden and maneuver wheelbarrows. For easy maintenance and weeding, the garden beds were kept small, yet they contained many plant varieties which produced an impressive amount of flowers and vegetables. Corn, sunflowers and zinnias were planted around the outside perimeter to give the garden an enclosed, "secret garden" feeling. The interior was laid out with inviting narrow paths and large open areas for easy access to the compost bin and cowboy hose holder. Although the props are fanciful, each one is functional. For example, we were unable to eat all the lettuce that grew in the hull of the sailboat; the wagon carried a full load of produce and flowers all summer and then displayed our gourds and pumpkins in the fall; and the sundial faithfully ticked off the hours of the day.

Most importantly, the Family Garden provides a place where adults and children can work, play, explore and learn together. It's not necessary to recreate this garden in its entirety to enjoy these experiences. Your family will have fun assembling any one of these projects in your own backyard garden.

Dolphins swimming alongside the sailboat

Front view of the Family Garden

Children harvesting squash and sampling red, ripe tomatoes

Vegetable bed filled with kohlrabi, broccoli and cabbages

The garden in early autumn

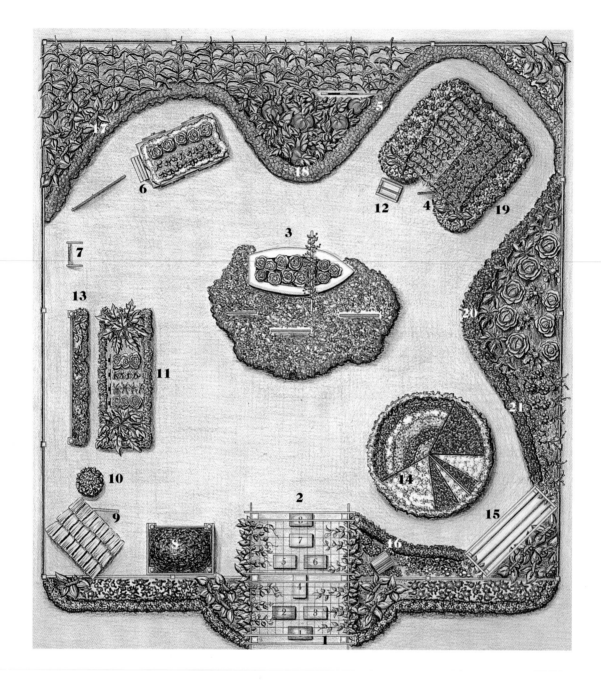

Family Garden Plan

1. Arbor
2. Hopscotch
3. Sailboat and Dolphins
4. Bean House
5. Scarecrow
6. Horse-Drawn Wagon
7. Cowboy

8. Compost Bin
9. Garden Shed
10. Topiary
11. Row Markers
12. Plant Caddy
13. Vegetable Trellis
14. Sundial

15. Garden Bench
16. Bird Feeder
17. Sunflowers
18. Pumpkins
19. Edible Flowers
20. Vegetables
21. Dried Flowers

Part Two

Garden Projects

Project Basics

Before You Begin

The following projects will come together smoothly if you follow the instructions and adhere to these few simple rules:

1. Safety is the number-one rule. This book advocates family participation in the construction of these projects; however, you must use common sense. Parental supervision is suggested at all times. Children should never use dangerous power tools and toxic chemicals (such as paints, thinners, lacquers, etc.). Allow your children to participate by giving them age-appropriate tasks that are easy and safe for them to perform. Very young children may have to wait until the projects are complete before they can participate by digging and playing in the garden. These projects are meant as garden decorations only and should not be used as playground equipment.

2. Thoroughly read and understand the instructions before you begin each project.

3. Assemble all the required materials before you begin.

4. Have fun!

Enlarging and Transferring Patterns

The patterns in this book must be enlarged and transferred to pattern paper. Pattern paper can be any inexpensive paper such as butcher paper, craft paper, or roll-end newsprint. Several of the projects require large patterns so it may be necessary to tape several pieces of paper together.

One of three methods can be used to enlarge and transfer the patterns from the book to your pattern paper:

Method 1

Use the measurement given next to the grid and pattern piece in the book to create an enlarged grid on your pattern paper. For example, if one square of the grid = 1 inch, use a pencil and ruler to create a grid on your pattern paper with 1-inch squares. Once your ruled grid is complete, transfer the drawing in the book to your enlarged grid by carefully drawing the pattern piece, square by square, onto your pattern paper.

Method 2

This method will require an opaque projector (often available for rent from art and graphic supply stores). Tape pattern paper to a far wall. Place the book in the opaque projector and adjust the projector's distance from the wall until the projected grid becomes the correct measurement for that pattern. Trace the projection onto the pattern paper with a pencil (a marker might bleed through to the wall paint).

Method 3

For small pattern pieces, use a photocopy machine to enlarge the patterns.

Transfer Paper

Many of the wooden cutout projects in this book require that painting guidelines be transferred from your enlarged paper patterns onto the wooden cutout. This can easily be done with transfer paper. Various types of transfer paper, such as carbon or graphite paper, are available at office, craft and art supply stores. If you use carbon paper, do a test on a small block of wood in order to make sure the carbon lines won't bleed through your paint. Graphite transfer paper should not bleed. In the following text, the term carbon paper is used to represent all types of transfer paper.

ARBOR

The gourd arbor creates the grand entrance to the garden

A well-placed arbor can be as beautiful as it is functional. Small gardens will benefit from an arbor's vertical growing area; sprawling vines can grow up rather than out. Covered in vigorous gourd vines, this arbor creates a grand entrance to the Family Garden. The leafy screen not only provides a shady place to rest and play, but also a bountiful harvest of gourds for craft projects.

MATERIALS LIST

A – posts	3½" × 3½" × 120"	(6)	treated 4×4
B – support boards	1½" × 5½" × 120"	(2)	standard 2×6
C – spanner boards	1½" × 5½" × 96"	(6)	standard 2×6
D – brace boards	1½" × 5½" × 39¾"	(2)	standard 2×6
E – screen boards	1½" × 1½" × 84"	(16)	standard 2×2
F – arbor screens	41¼" × 19' 8"	(2)	48" × 50' roll, 2×4 mesh welded-wire fencing

8d galvanized box nails

12d galvanized box nails

wire staples

exterior primer/sealer

exterior paint

ASSEMBLY INSTRUCTIONS

1. Begin construction of the arbor by cutting all the lumber to size, as given in the materials list. Use the grid in Fig. 1 to mark the ends of the support and spanner boards. Cut with a saber saw and sand the ends smooth.

2. In the location where you are going to construct the arbor, measure off a 6 × 8-foot rectangle with stakes and string. The placement of the six upright posts (**A**) is very important, so you'll want to carefully check your measurements.

3. Dig four post holes 2 feet deep at the inside four corners of the rectangle, and two more holes midpoint along the two 8-foot sides, see Fig. 2.

4. Take your time to set these six posts. They should extend 8 feet above the ground, with their tops level to each other. Once all six posts are plumb and level, fill and tamp the dirt around the base of the posts. For extra support you might want to add cement to the base of each post, below ground level.

5. The first boards you will install are the two 10-foot support boards (**B**) which run the 8-foot length of the arbor and extend beyond both ends by 1 foot. Their top edges are 5½ inches below the top of the posts. Nail these boards in place, using the 12d galvanized box nails (for this, and subsequent steps, you will probably need the help of an assistant).

6. The next two boards you will nail in place are the two outermost spanner boards (**C**). These attach to the outside edge of both sets of entrance posts. Their top edges are level with the tops of the posts, and their ends extend beyond the posts by 1 foot. Don't nail in the four remaining spanner boards at this time.

7. The four remaining spanner boards are first

Arbor End Grid

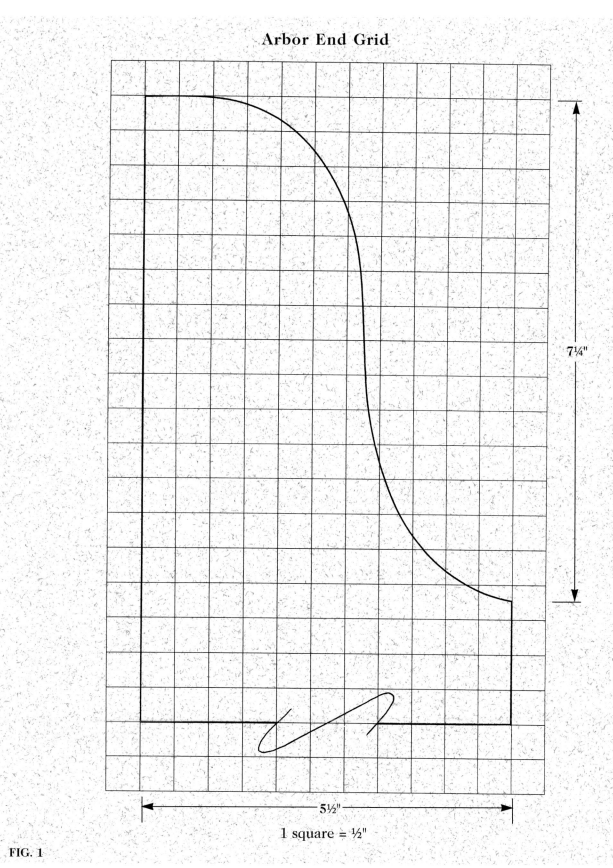

7¼"

5½"

1 square = ½"

FIG. 1

Full View of Arbor

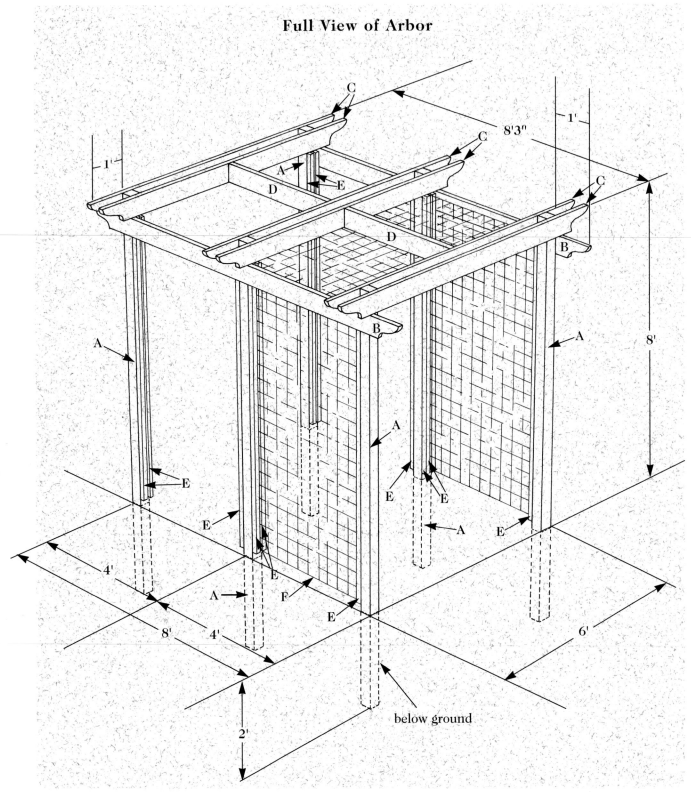

FIG. 2

Detail of Arbor Screen Assembly

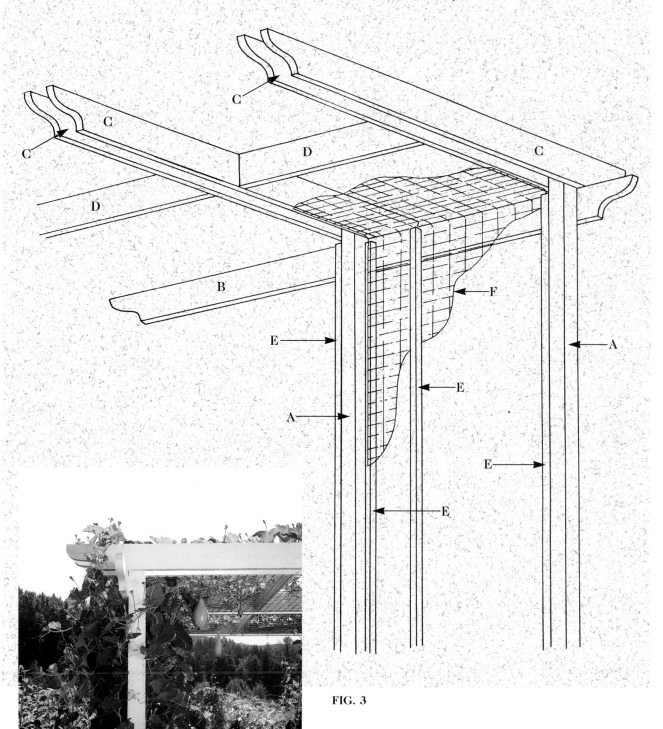

FIG. 3

*By midsummer the gourd vines totally
envelop the arbor*

Young gourds hanging from arbor's ceiling

combined with the two brace boards (**D**) to form a pair of "H" assemblies. Mark with a pencil the midpoints on all four spanner boards. Nail a brace board between two of the spanner boards at the midpoint so that the resulting assembly is in the shape of an "H". Repeat with the remaining two spanner boards. The reason for combining these boards on the ground is that, once the spanner boards are in place on the arbor, there would be no room to nail the two brace boards in place.

8. With the help of an assistant, lift each "H" assembly up into place, resting them on the two support boards. When you are done positioning them so that all the spanner boards line up 1 foot beyond the posts on each side, nail them to the posts with 12d galvanized box nails.

9. Prime and paint the entire arbor, including the screen boards (**E**).

10. Install the first eight screen boards as shown in Figs. 2 & 3. This first set is nailed onto the posts 1 inch below the spanner boards and approximately 5½ inches above the ground. They are also flush to the outside edges of the posts and become the stapling surface for the vertical edge of the arbor screen. Attach the screen boards using 8d galvanized box nails.

11. Once all eight screen boards are in place, cut to size both pieces of welded-wire fencing (**F**) as given in the materials list. Use a good pair of nail nippers to cut the fencing.

12. After you have cut the two sections of fencing, you will need to make two bends to create a "U" shape; see Fig. 2.

13. Start by measuring off 84 inches of length on the first screen. Place a 2×4 across the width of the screen and bend the section up. Try to make a good crease at the edge of the 2×4.

14. From the point of that first bend, continue measuring off another 69 inches and again make another crease, folding the last section of the screen upwards.

15. When finished, you should have a screen that measures 69 inches across the top, 84 inches on one side, and 83 inches on the other. Insert the screen into place in the arbor as shown in Fig. 3. The screen is secured to the arbor frame with fencing staples. The sides are stapled to the screen boards and the top is stapled to the underside of the brace and spanner boards.

16. After securing the first screen in place, repeat the same steps for the remaining screen.

17. Once both screens are installed, nail on the remaining eight screen boards as shown in Figs. 2 & 3. This second set of screen boards will shield the sharp ends of the fence wire, especially important with children using the arbor as a play area. It will also give the arbor a finished and tidy look.

HOPSCOTCH

Patiently waiting their turn

Hopping to and from the garden on these rainbow-colored paving stones will delight children and adults alike. The pavers offer a place to play while also providing dry footing along a well-traveled path. This project is easy and inexpensive to make, yet it will likely become one of the most often used items in your garden. The following instructions also include details for making a tossing beanbag. Unlike tossing pebbles in the game of hopscotch, the small beanbag lands easily on the squares without rolling off. This feature will make the game fun for even the youngest player.

MATERIALS LIST

cement patio pavers	1½" × 8" × 16"	(8)
exterior primer/sealer (suitable for use on masonry)		
polyurethane exterior gloss enamel paints (assorted colors)		
carbon paper		
sand		
mulch (sawdust, wood chips, ground bark, etc.)		
4-inch squares of fabric		(2)
½ cup dried beans or popcorn		

ASSEMBLY INSTRUCTIONS

Painting

1. If you purchased your pavers from a garden center, where they might have been stored outside and exposed to the rain, bring them indoors for two or three weeks until they dry completely.
2. Paint the primer/sealer over all surfaces of each block. Cement is porous, so make sure they are well sealed, even if it means applying a second coat. Let the primer dry completely between coats.
3. You can buy an assortment of enamel colors, or you can purchase just the primary colors (red, yellow and blue) and mix your own palette. Paint each paver a different color, applying two coats of paint to all surfaces of each paver. Again, let the paint dry completely between coats.

The hopscotch blocks create a rainbow pathway

Numbering

1. On eight separate sheets of paper, use a photocopy machine to enlarge each number in Fig. 4 to a height of 4½ inches (400 percent).

2. Lightly tape each numbered sheet of paper to a paver, carefully centering the numbers on each block. Note that all the blocks are positioned horizontally with the exception of paver number four which is placed vertically (see photo). Position the numbers on the blocks accordingly.

3. Carefully lift the tape along one edge of the paper and slip a piece of carbon paper between the paver and the numbered sheet (carbon side facing the paver). Trace around the outside edge of each number. As you trace, occasionally lift a corner of the paper and carbon to make sure you are pressing hard enough to leave a carbon line drawing. Remove the paper and carbon from the blocks.

4. With white enamel paint, a small brush and a steady hand, paint the numbers, staying within the carbon lines. Two coats of paint may be necessary. Wait until the numbers are dry before placing the pavers in the garden.

Installation in the Garden

Prepare the garden area for the blocks by leveling the ground using a square shovel and a hard rake. To prevent the blocks from rocking as the children jump, evenly spread a 1-inch layer of sand

Hopscotch Numbers

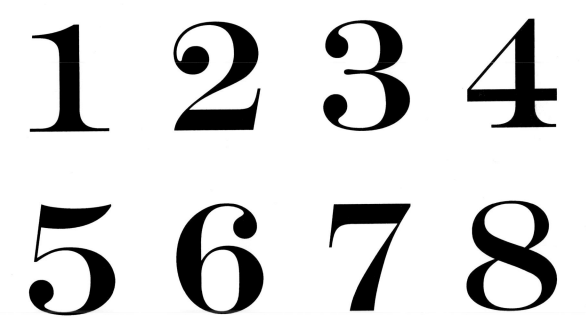

FIG. 4

over the area. Set the pavers into place measuring equal distances between them and leveling each block. Secure the blocks by adding additional sand between the pavers and finish the project off with a surrounding layer of mulch.

To prolong the life of the painted numbers, store the hopscotch blocks in a garage or basement during the wet and frosty winter months.

Tossing Beanbag

To make a tossing beanbag, start with two 4-inch squares of fabric. With right sides together, sew a ¼-inch seam around three sides of the square. Turn the bag right-side-out and press. Press under the open edge ¼ inch. Fill the bag half full with dried beans or popcorn seeds. Slipstitch the opening closed.

Tossing bean bags make the game fun and easy

SAILBOAT AND DOLPHINS

This garden boat sails on a sea of lobelia

"Floating" in a sea of deep blue lobelia, this garden boat has a full sail of scarlet runner beans and its hull is planted to capacity with several varieties of lettuce. With dolphins frolicking off the bow and stern, what child wouldn't be charmed by this fanciful, edible ship?

MATERIALS LIST

Sailboat

A – posts	3½" × 3½" × 36"	(5)	treated 4×4
B – side walls	¾" × 5½" × 36"	(6)	cedar 1×6
C – bow walls	¾" × 5½" × 33¾"	(6)	cedar 1×6
D – stern walls	¾" × 5½" × 22½"	(3)	cedar 1×6
E – bow nailing strip	¾" × 1½" × 16"	(1)	cedar 1×2
F – bow extension	1½" × 1½" × 16"	(1)	cedar 2×2
G – mast board	¾" × 5½" × 21¾"	(1)	cedar 1×6
H – side ribs	¼" × 4" × trim to length	(8–12)	cedar bender board
I – stern ribs	¼" × 4" × 25"	(4–6)	cedar bender board
J – side gunnels	¾" × 5½" × 37¼"	(2)	pine or fir 1×6
K – bow gunnels	¾" × 9½" × 43¼"	(2)	pine or fir 1×10
L – stern gunnel	¾" × 5½" × 22½"	(1)	pine or fir 1×6
M – bow triangle	¾" × 2" × 3"	(1)	pine or fir
N – mast	3" × 96"	(1)	treated fence post
O – mast finial		(1)	fence post finial
P – mast spar	¾" × 60"	(1)	PVC schedule 40
Q – spar caps	¾"	(2)	PVC schedule 40
R – bow trim	¼" × 1½" × 16"	(2)	cedar lath

12' of 17-gauge fence wire	(6)
small screw eyes	(2)
3d galvanized box nails	
8d galvanized box nails	
¾" × #6 galvanized wood screws	
exterior primer/sealer	
exterior paint	

The cargo contains several varieties of lettuce

Plants

Lettuce (red leaf, green leaf, endive)	(9)
Scarlet runner beans	(12)
Lobelia (1-inch plugs)	(300) (approx. 4½ flats)

Dolphin

A – taller head	¾" × 16" × 32"	(1)	¾" ACX plywood
B – shorter head	¾" × 14" × 32"	(1)	¾" ACX plywood
C – fin	¾" × 14" × 24"	(1)	¾" ACX plywood

10' × ½" EMT thin-wall metal conduit	(1)
½" conduit pipe straps	(10)
¾" × #6 galvanized wood screws	(20)
exterior primer/sealer	
exterior polyurethane	
acrylic craft paints (black, white and medium gray)	
carbon paper	

ASSEMBLY INSTRUCTIONS

Sailboat

1. Sail into this project by cutting to size the lumber given in the materials list. Using the grids to make patterns of all the gunnel pieces, trace and cut to size (remember that after you trace out one side of the bow or side gunnels, you must flip over the pattern to make its match for the opposite side); see Figs. 5–8. Throughout this project the front of the boat is referred to as the bow, and the rear of the boat is referred to as the stern.

2. In the area where you will be placing the boat, mark the position of each post (**A**); see Fig. 9. Dig five post holes to a depth of 20 inches each. Install the five posts and level them to each other. When all five posts are level and in the proper position, fill in the loose dirt around the posts and tamp the ground firm.

3. Across the inside edges of the rear two posts, install the three stern wall boards (**D**) with 8d galvanized box nails; see Fig. 10.

4. Next, install the six side wall boards (**B**) between the two rear posts and the two mid-posts. Notice that the side wall boards nail onto the *outside* of the rear posts, but onto the *inside* of the mid-posts; see Fig. 10.

5. Before you can install the bow side walls (**C**), you need to nail on the bow nailing strip (**E**). Then, toenail in place the six remaining bow walls to complete the basic inside frame of the sailboat planter box; see Fig. 10.

6. Nail the bow extension (**F**) on the front of the bow post at this time. This board will provide a nailing surface for the sailboat's side ribs; see Fig. 10.

7. Now set the mast board (**G**) across the top of the bow walls just to the front of the mid-posts; see Fig. 10. You will need to notch both sides of the top bow wall boards so the mast board sits in

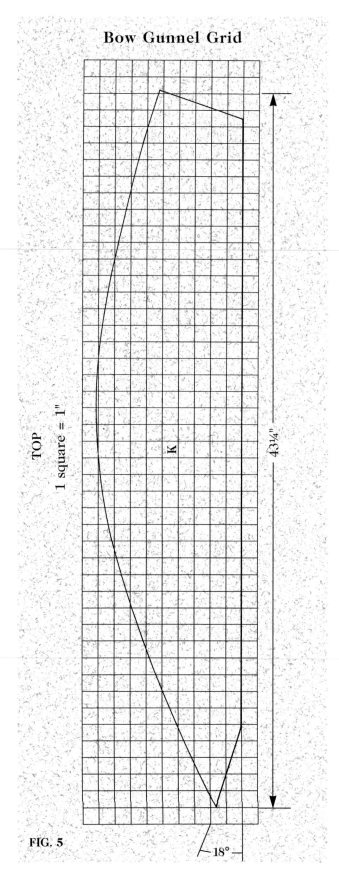

Bow Gunnel Grid

TOP

'1 square = 1"

K

4¾"

FIG. 5

∟18°

Side Gunnel Grid

TOP
1 square = 1"

2"

J

37¼"

5½"

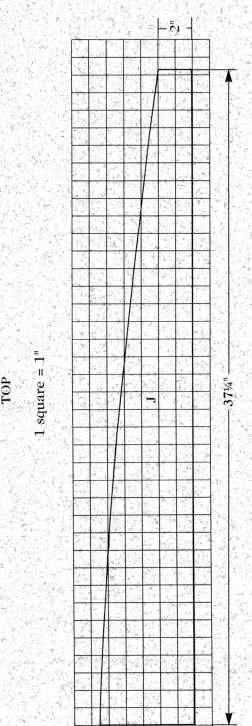

FIG. 6

Stern Gunnel Grid

5½"

TOP
1 square = 1"

L

22½"

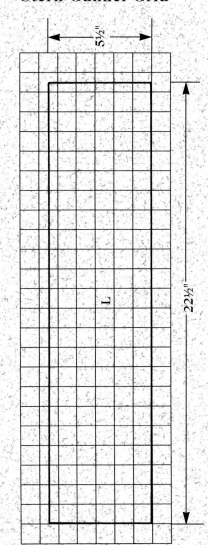

FIG. 7

Bow Triangle Grid

1 square = 1"

M

3"

2"

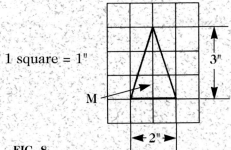

FIG. 8

Boat Frame Top View

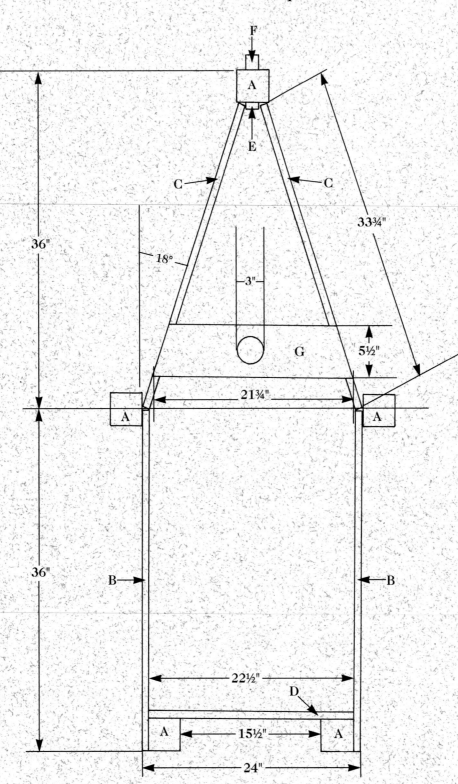

FIG. 9

Boat Frame

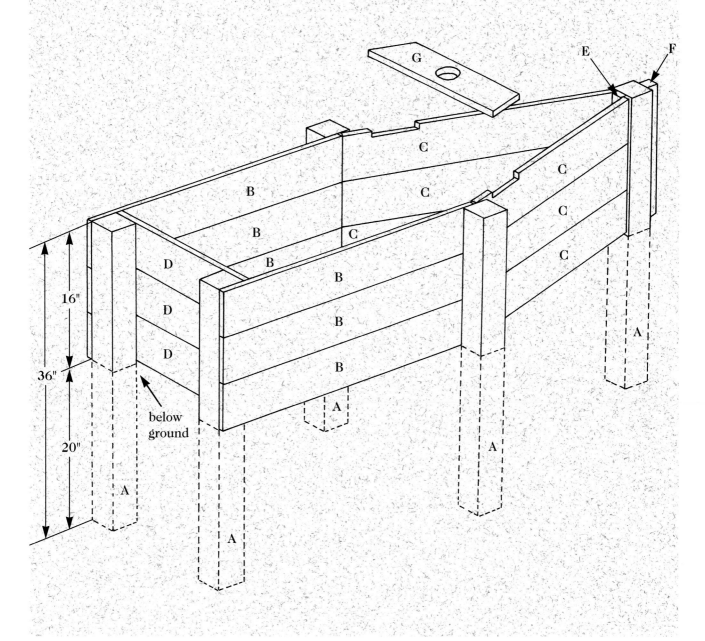

FIG. 10

flush with the top edge. Mark the notch location on the two top bow wall boards with a pencil. Also mark the underside of the mast board where it overhangs the bow walls. Trim the mast board and notch both sides of the bow walls with a saber saw or chisel.

8. Before installing the mast board, cut a 3-inch diameter hole at the center, to accept the mast. Set the mast board in place and mark the ground directly below the hole. Remove the mast board and dig a 2-foot-deep post hole at your mark. Now drill three holes in the mast pole (**N**): a 1⅛-inch hole for the spar, a ⅜-inch hole for the spar wires to go through and a ¼-inch hole in the top of the mast for the finial screw; see Fig. 11. Mount the mast finial (**O**) to the top of the mast pole. Then, nail in place the mast board and install the mast (make sure the spar hole runs perpendicular to the sides of the boat). Fill in the dirt around the mast pole and tamp firm.

9. The side ribs (**H**) of the sailboat are made from common bender board. When choosing the bender boards for this project, try to pick boards that are between ⅛ inch and ¼ inch in thickness and free of any large knots. The ribs are "shingled" up the sides of the boat. You will need between 4 and 6 bender boards per side, depending on their width and how much you overlap them. An exact measurement was left off the length of the side ribs in the materials list because it will vary depending on how the boards bend. Therefore, test and pencil-mark each board for proper length before cutting.

10. Nail on the side ribs starting at the bottom stern of the boat. Attach the first piece of bender board to the rear post using a 3d galvanized box nail; see Fig. 12. Nail all the bender board about 1 inch from the top edge so the bottom edge can flex out if necessary. As you bend the board past the mid-post, secure it with another nail. Finally, bend the board to a point directly in front of the bow extension board. Nail this end to the exten-

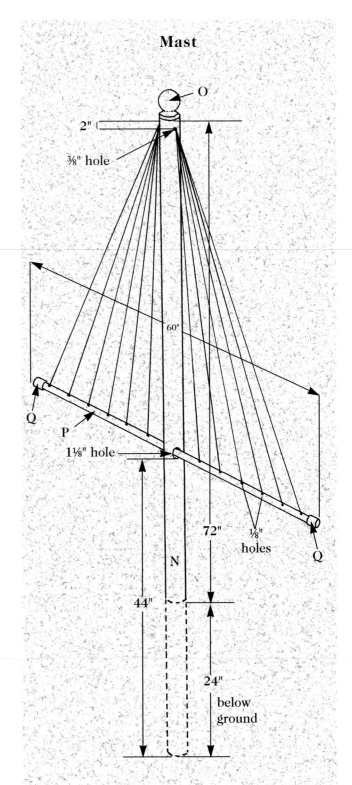

FIG. 11

Side and Stern Ribs

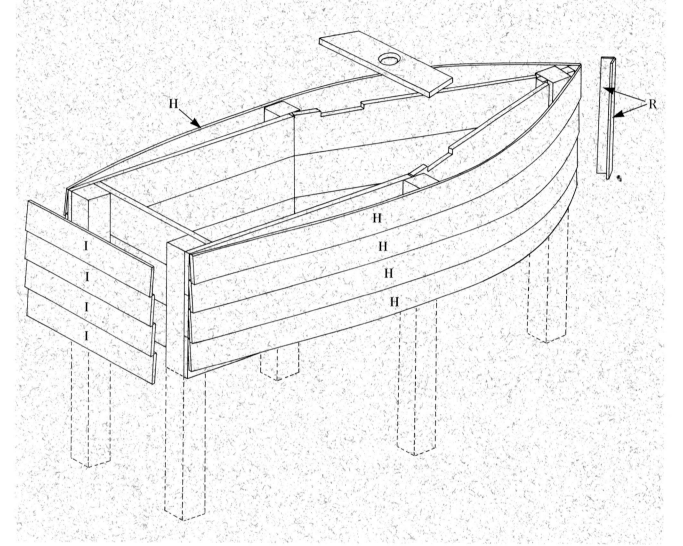

FIG. 12

Gunnel Boards

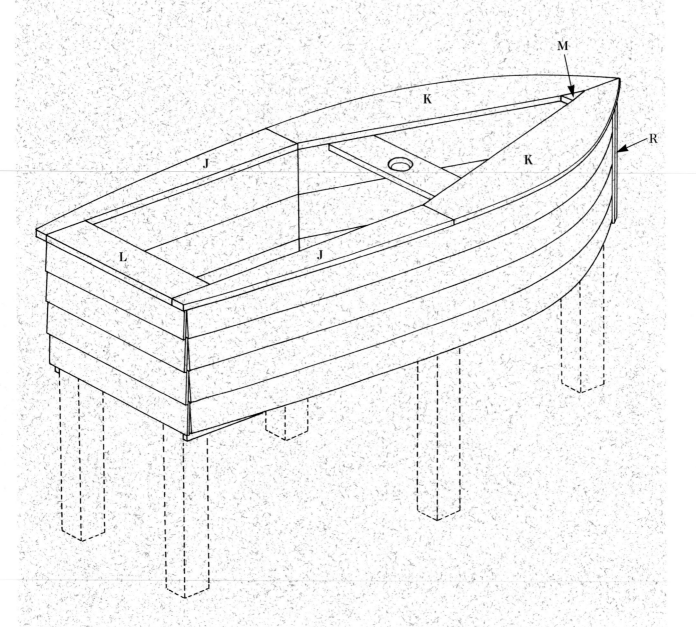

FIG. 13

sion board or the bow post. Repeat the same procedure as you install all the ribs on each side of the boat. Space the overlap so that the last board is flush with the top of the posts.

11. The steps are basically the same for the stern. However, because there is no bending involved, you can pre-cut all of these rib pieces. Install the stern rib boards (**I**) at this time.

12. Now you are ready to attach the six gunnel boards. When in place they should overhang the boat ribs by about 1 inch. First, nail in place the two bow gunnel boards (**K**) using 8d galvanized finish nails; see Fig. 13. The bow gunnels nail into the bow posts and mid-posts, as well as along the top edge of the bow walls.

13. Next, nail in place the two side gunnels (**J**). Again, nail along the top of the side walls as well as into the mid-posts.

14. The stern gunnel (**L**) goes on next and, like the other gunnel boards, lines up along the inside edge of the planter box wall. Nail it to the two stern posts as well as along the stern wall.

15. Next, install the bow triangle (**M**). This piece is simply designed to cover up the nailing strip (**E**) and bow post, which are still visible. Pre-drill this piece to avoid splitting the wood.

16. Attach the two bow trim pieces (**R**) using two ¾" × #6 galvanized wood screws to secure each side; see Figs. 12 & 13.

17. Now, complete the mast by drilling twelve ⅛-inch holes through the mast spar (**P**). Space them evenly, six on each side of the mast, leaving room for the two end caps. Install the spar through the 1⅛-inch hole in the mast. Slip the end caps (**Q**) over the open ends of the spar.

18. On one side of the mast, thread the six wires individually through the ⅛-inch holes in the spar and twist the ends back around themselves. Feed all six wires through the ⅜-inch hole at the top of the mast. Attach them in the same manner to their matching holes on the other side of the spar; see Fig. 11. Trim off any excess wire.

19. Install two small screw-eyes in the bow gunnels, just below the spar. Secure the spar to the screw-eyes with two short lengths of wire.

20. Apply a coat of primer/sealer to all surfaces and finish with two coats of the exterior paint in your choice of colors.

A billowing sail of scarlet runner beans

Planting Instructions

Once the boat is complete, fill the hull with a mixture of topsoil, peat, well-rotted manure and compost. Plant a row of scarlet runner beans across the width of the boat along the rear of the mast board. Plant the remainder of the hull with a variety of lettuce or a mixture of any low-growing vegetables. As the bean vines grow, you may need to twist-tie some of them along the spar so the outermost wires will be covered in vines (left on their own they will grow straight up the mast). Once the vines are long enough, they can be encouraged to wind up the individual sail wires.

To create the lobelia "water," start by determining the perimeter of the "sea." Lay a garden hose on the ground and gently curve it around the front side of the boat. The lobelia "sea" pictured is approximately 132 inches in length and 90 inches from the edge of the boat to the perimeter (for easy harvesting access, the back of the boat is not planted with lobelia). Loosen and amend the soil within the boundaries of the hose and rake the soil smooth. Plant the 1-inch lobelia plugs approximately 8 inches apart across the prepared soil (see Sow Your Own Plug Flats on page 135).

ASSEMBLY INSTRUCTIONS

Dolphin

1. Begin by enlarging the grid patterns for the dolphin heads and fin onto two separate pieces of pattern paper; see Figs. 14A & 14B. Use the same grid pattern for both dolphin heads, making one head 2 inches shorter than the other by cutting along the dashed line. This will give the effect of one dolphin being lower in the "water." Include all the painting guidelines for the eyes and mouth on the enlarged pattern. Once the patterns are complete, use scissors to carefully cut around the outline of the pattern pieces.

2. Lay the plywood sheets across two sawhorses, sanded side up. Place and lightly tape the two paper patterns to the plywood. With a pencil, draw around the outside edges of the pattern pieces leaving a penciled outline on the wood. Remove the pattern pieces. Repeat the process for the second dolphin head.

3. With a saber saw, cut the plywood along the penciled outlines. Finish by sanding all surfaces and edges smooth.

A dolphin frolicking off the bow

Dolphin Fin Grid

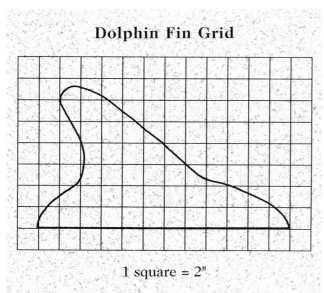

1 square = 2"

FIG. 14A

Dolphin Head Grid

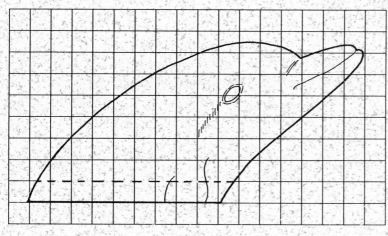

1 square = 2"

FIG. 14B

*Painting detail
of the dolphin*

4. Paint two coats of exterior primer to the front, back and edges of each cutout. Let the primer dry completely between coats.

5. Then paint two coats of medium-gray acrylic paint to the front, back and edges of each cutout. Again, let the paint dry completely between applying coats.

6. Re-tape the dolphin head pattern to the front side of the plywood cutout. Lifting the tape when necessary, slip a piece of carbon paper between the pattern piece and the plywood cutout (carbon side facing the plywood). With a pencil, trace over the painting guidelines leaving a carbon-line drawing on the painted surface. Remove the pattern from the plywood and repeat the process for the second dolphin head.

7. On a ceramic plate or an enamel mixing tray, place a generous amount of gray, black and white acrylic paint. Mix portions of these three paints together to create the shadows and highlights along the dolphin bodies. For example, mix a small amount of white with the gray to make a lighter shade of gray. This shade can be brushed along the top line of the fin and heads to create a highlight. Mix a small amount of black with the gray to make a darker shade of gray. This shade can be applied around their mouths and under their chins to create areas of shadow. As you paint, blend the highlights and shadows into the color of your medium gray base coat. Use the photos as a guide.

8. Using the painting guidelines, complete the detail painting by defining each dolphin mouth with dark gray paint and adding their eyes. The eyes are easily created by painting a solid black oval and then adding a curved white line at the top of the eye and a curved dark gray line at the bottom of the eye. See the photos for further details.

9. Complete the project by sealing all edges and surfaces with two protective coats of exterior polyurethane.

Installation in the Garden

Cut the 10-foot piece of conduit into five 2-foot pieces with a hacksaw (two for each head and one for the fin). Using the dolphin heads and fin as a guide, drive the conduit pipes into the ground about 1 foot deep so they are hidden behind the cutouts. Then attach the cutouts to the conduit pipes with the ten pipe straps and twenty ¾" × #6 galvanized wood screws; see Fig. 15.

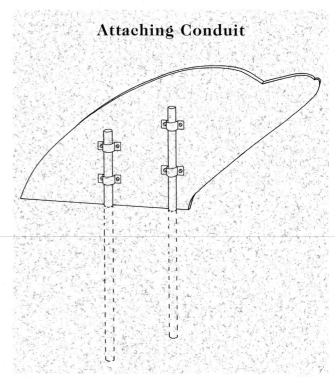

Attaching Conduit

FIG. 15

At summer's end, store the dolphins in a garage or basement for the winter months. In the spring, be sure to apply an additional protective coat of polyurethane before you set them out in the garden.

BEAN HOUSE

By midsummer the house is covered in vines providing a shady place for children

A tiny Tudor cottage, with a door small enough to discourage most adults from entering, is just the kind of hideaway children love. Every year, your children can grow their own edible playhouse. By midsummer, the walls and roof of the cottage become totally enclosed with bean vines and the surrounding "landscape" is filled with edible flowers. The bean house is not only an engaging place to play, but it also becomes a portion of your dinner!

MATERIALS LIST

Wood Facade

A – frame piece	¾" × 3½" × 48"	(2)	pine or fir 1×4
B – frame piece	¾" × 3½" × 44½"	(2)	pine or fir 1×4
C – frame piece	¾" × 3½" × 41"	(1)	pine or fir 1×4
D – frame piece	¾" × 3½" × 30⅜"	(1)	pine or fir 1×4
E – frame piece	¾" × 3½" × 33⅞"	(1)	pine or fir 1×4
F – frame piece	¾" × 3½" × 8"	(2)	pine or fir 1×4
G – frame piece	¾" × 3½" × 18"	(1)	pine or fir 1×4
H – roof trim	¾" × 2½" × 35¾"	(2)	pine or fir 1×3
I – side trim	¾" × 1½" × 48"	(2)	pine or fir 1×2
J – front panel	½" × 48" × 72"	(1)	½" ACX plywood
K – door panel	½" × 18" × 36"	(1)	½" ACX plywood (cut from front panel)

1" × #8 galvanized wood screws

2" strap hinges with mounting screws

gate hook-and-eye set

6d galvanized finish nails

3d galvanized finish nails

small can wood filler

exterior primer/sealer

exterior polyurethane

assorted acrylic craft paints

exterior brown paint

*Bean vines wind their way up the walls
and roof in early summer*

PVC Frame

A – frame pipe	¾" × 60"	(6)	schedule 40
B – frame pipe	¾" × 28⅛"	(4)	schedule 40
C – frame pipe	¾" × 41¼"	(2)	schedule 40
D – frame pipe	¾" × 38⅝"	(2)	schedule 40
E – frame pipe	¾" × 44⅛"	(1)	schedule 40
F – frame pipe	¾" × 2⅛"	(4)	schedule 40
G – frame pipe	¾" × 1¼"	(10)	schedule 40

¾" tee couplings	(14)
¾" 45-degree elbow couplings	(4)
¾" 90-degree elbow couplings	(2)
¾" pipe straps w/screws	(6)
small can PVC cement primer	
small can PVC cement	
½" × 10' EMT thin-wall metal conduit	(1)
220' 17-gauge fencing wire	

Plant List

Dwarf sunflowers	(6)
Violas	(16)
Nasturtiums	(6)
Calendulas	(35)
Romano pole beans	(28)

ASSEMBLY INSTRUCTIONS

Wood Facade

1. Cut to size the wood pieces given in the materials list. Use the grid in Fig. 16 to cut the door (**K**) from the main sheet of 4×6-foot ACX plywood. The roof slope (**J**) and roof trim (**H**) is cut to a 45-degree angle, as shown in Fig. 17.

2. Attach the bracing boards (**A**) (**B**) (**C**) (**D**) (**E**) (**F**) (**G**) to the back of the facade using the 1-inch galvanized wood screws; see Fig. 18. The screws are inserted through pre-drilled and countersunk holes in the front of the plywood facade so they can be filled and sanded later.

3. After the bracing boards are secured to the back of the facade, miter and attach the two roof trim and two side trim pieces (**H**) (**I**) with 6d galvanized finish nails. The roof trim pieces overhang the face of the house by ¾ inch. The side trim pieces are nailed flush to the face of the house.

4. Fill the screw and nail holes with wood filler and sand the entire facade including the trim and the door.

5. Paint the facade and door with two liberal coats of the white exterior latex primer.

6. After priming the facade, attach the door to the house face with the two strap hinges. Make sure the door is aligned properly to open and close without rubbing.

7. Install the hook-and-eye set.

Painting the Wood Facade

1. Begin by painting the back of the facade and door with two coats of exterior brown paint. Then enlarge the Tudor facade grid pattern onto a sheet of pattern paper; see Fig. 16. Include all the painting guidelines. Once the pattern is complete, use scissors to carefully cut around the outline of the pattern piece.

2. Lay the primed facade, front side up, across two sawhorses. Place and lightly tape the pattern cutout to the facade. Lifting the tape when necessary, slip a piece of carbon paper between the pattern piece and the facade (carbon side facing the plywood). With a pencil, trace over the painting guidelines leaving a carbon line drawing on the primed surface. Start by tracing over the large color-block areas such as beams and windows (leave off the fine detail items such as the white window-pane dividers and the hinges until step 4). Remove the pattern piece from the facade.

Painting detail of the bean house

Facade Grid

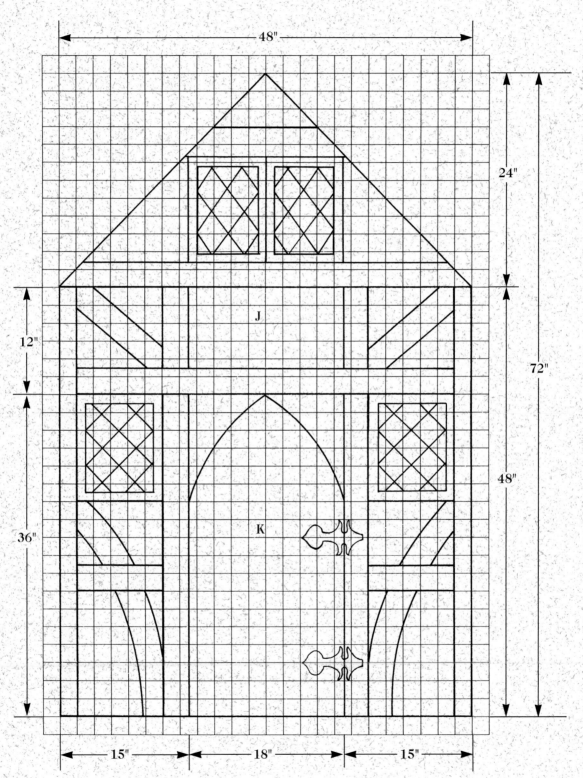

48"

24"

72"

12"

48"

36"

J

K

15"

18"

15"

FIG. 16

1 square = 2"

Front of Facade

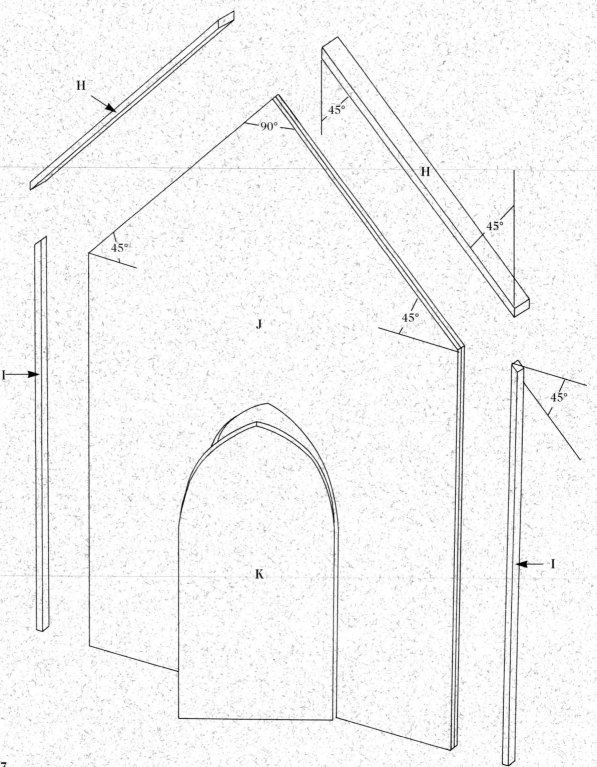

Back of Facade

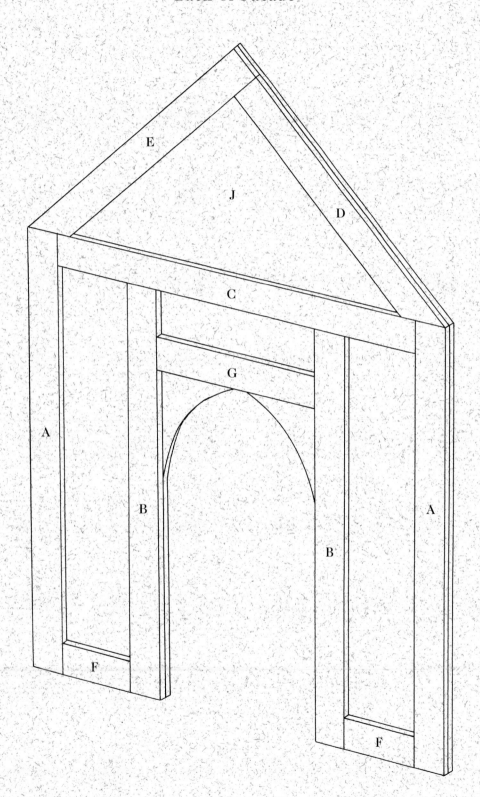

FIG. 18

3. Using your assortment of acrylic paints, paint in the large color-block areas. For example, use medium brown for the door, window frames and beams; light blue-gray for the windows; and creamy-yellow for the background.

4. When these painted areas are dry, re-tape the pattern piece to the facade. Once again, slip the carbon paper between the pattern and the cutout, this time tracing over the detail painting guidelines such as the hinges and the white windowpane dividers. Remove the pattern piece from the facade.

5. With your acrylic paints, paint in as much or as little detail as you wish. Optional details include wood grain, shadow areas under the beams and mottling on the wall surfaces (mottling can be easily done with a sponge).

6. Once the detail painting is finished, completely seal the facade by painting two protective coats of exterior polyurethane to the front, back and all edges.

PVC Frame

1. After completing the wood facade, you are ready to build the PVC frame. It consists of two end frames linked together by six pipes, each 5 feet long (A); see Fig. 19.

2. On a table or set of sawhorses, lay the facade face down and use the back as a base to lay out the pipes for gluing.

3. Assemble the front frame that will attach to the bracing boards on the back of the facade. The front frame does not have the lower cross pipe (E). Assemble the pieces without cementing them to make sure they line up properly. Once they are lined up, cement them in place.

4. Now assemble the rear frame using the same procedure. The rear frame has the lower cross pipe (E).

5. With both end frames completed, link them together with the six 5-foot pipes (A).

6. Use the 17-gauge wire to create a trellis for the beans (you can use string; however, it has a tendency to sag). To prevent the wires from sliding on the frame, drill 1/8-inch holes every 6 inches along the ridge pipes (A) and along the roof pipes (B) of the rear frame. Measure and cut the wire to the proper lengths as you work. Wrap and twist one end of the wire around the bottom pipe of the frame (A) (E). Secure the other end to the top ridge pipes by threading the wire through the 1/8-inch hole and twisting the end back around itself.

Assembly in the Garden

1. With completion of the wood facade and PVC frame, you are ready to assemble both parts in the garden. In the area of the garden where you plan to locate the house, prepare the soil by cultivating, amending and raking it smooth.

2. Set the PVC frame in position and lightly push down on the corners so they leave an impression in the soil. Set the frame aside.

3. Cut the 10-foot piece of conduit into four equal lengths (30 inches each). Pound them into the ground where the four corner pipes left an impression. Leave about 1 foot of each pipe aboveground.

4. Lift the PVC frame and set it down so that the four pieces of conduit slip up inside the four PVC pipe ends. This will add stability to the house.

5. Finally, attach the facade to the front PVC frame with the six evenly spaced pipe straps.

Pipe Frame

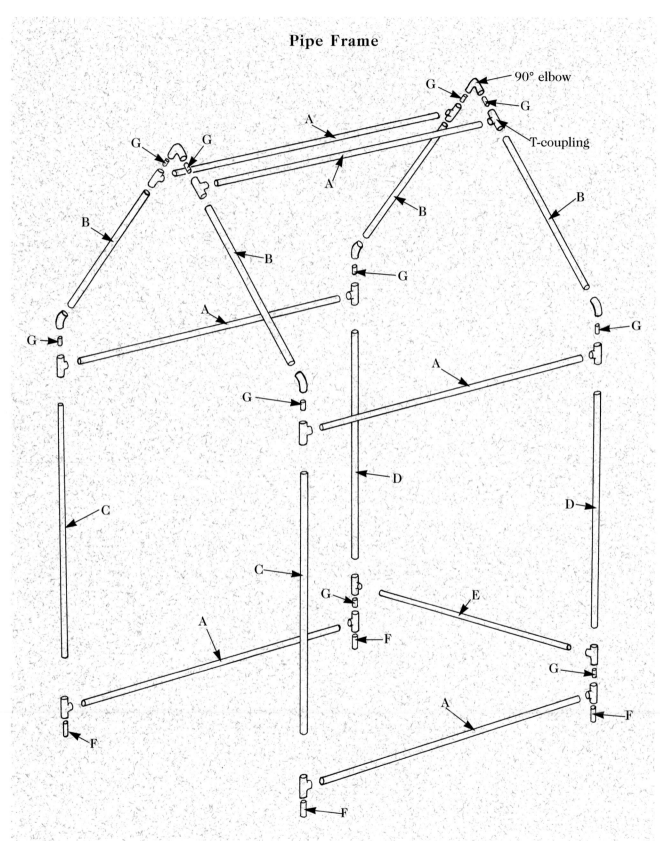

FIG. 19

Planting Instructions

In the spring, when all danger from frost has passed, your children can plant bean seeds around the base of the house. Romano pole beans were used to cover the bean house in the photo, but any pole bean will work. Following the instructions on the seed packet, plant one seed every 6 inches below the trellis wires. Bean seeds sprout quickly, so if some seeds don't germinate you will have plenty of time to re-plant extra seeds in the bare spots. By midsummer the bean vines should completely cover the house, providing a shady hideaway for children to play in and enjoy.

Edible-flower landscape

To complete this nourishing bean house, add a mini-landscape of edible flowers. Plant the borders with sunflowers, violas, calendulas and nasturtiums, which will provide colorful blooms all summer long. (For warnings, recipes and specific species suitable for use as edible flowers, see pages 148–149.)

At the end of summer, disassemble the facade from the PVC frame and store the facade only in a garage or basement for the winter months. Then, in the spring, apply an additional coat of polyurethane to the bean house before setting it back out in the garden.

SCARECROW

This scarecrow is too friendly to shoo away the crows

A well-placed scarecrow is the finishing touch to any vegetable garden, and your personal Family Garden is no exception. This friendly scarecrow may not safeguard your corn; however, she's always available to offer a helping hand. Standing four feet tall, her outstretched arms can hold the handle of an empty watering can, a harvest basket or your sweater when the afternoon sun becomes too hot. Young gardeners delight in this life-size garden companion.

MATERIALS LIST

Scarecrow	¾" × 48" × 54"	(1)	¾" ACX plywood
½" × 10' EMT thin-wall metal conduit		(1)	
½" pipe straps		(4)	
¾" × #6 galvanized wood screws		(8)	
exterior primer/sealer			
brown exterior paint			
exterior polyurethane			
acrylic craft paints (assorted colors)			
15' × ¼" rope			
carbon paper			

*Holding a sweater or an empty harvest basket is
this scarecrow's specialty*

ASSEMBLY INSTRUCTIONS

1. Begin by enlarging the grid pattern for the scarecrow's body onto a large piece of pattern paper; see Fig. 20. Include all the painting guidelines with the exception of her facial details. Use the close-up grid of her face and trace it onto your enlarged paper pattern; see Fig. 21. Once the pattern is enlarged, use scissors to carefully cut out the paper pattern around the outside edge and the interior cut-out area between the scarecrow's arm and the crow's tail.

2. Lay the sheet of ¾-inch plywood across two sawhorses, sanded-side-up. Place and lightly tape the paper pattern cutout to the plywood. With a pencil, draw around the pattern piece leaving a penciled outline on the wood. Remove the pattern from the wood.

3. With a saber saw, cut the plywood along the pencil line. In the cut-out area between the crow's tail and the scarecrow's arm, drill a ⅜-inch hole to allow access with the saw blade. The space between the crow's legs is not cut out, it is solid wood painted white. Finish by sanding all the surfaces and edges smooth.

4. Paint two coats of exterior primer to the front, back and edges of the cutout. Let the primer dry completely between coats. Paint the back of the

Scarecrow Grid

1 square = 2"

FIG. 20

scarecrow with two coats of exterior brown paint.

5. Re-tape the paper pattern piece to the primed cutout. Lifting the tape when necessary, slip a piece of carbon paper between the pattern piece and the plywood cutout (carbon side facing the plywood). With a pencil, trace over the painting guidelines leaving a carbon line drawing on the primed surface. Start by tracing over the large color-block areas such as the scarecrow's pants, shirt, head, hat, gloves and crow (leave off the fine detail items, such as buttons, pockets and straw, until step 7). Remove the pattern piece from the plywood.

6. Using acrylic paints, paint in the large color-block areas. For example, use light brown paint to block in the trousers, green for the shirt, red for the hat, tan for her burlap head, cream for the gloves and black for the crow. As an optional detail, paint in shadows or highlights at this time. For example, on her shirt, apply a slightly darker shade of green under her arms and a slightly lighter shade of green to her shoulders and the upper side of her arms.

Painting detail of the scarecrow's shirt

See photos for details.

7. When the paint is dry, re-tape the paper pattern piece to the cutout. Once again, slip the carbon paper between the pattern and the cutout, this time tracing over the detail painting guidelines (these include pockets, buttons, facial features, straw, patches, the crow's wing, etc.). With your assortment of acrylic paint colors, paint in as much or as little detail as you wish. For example, with a small brush, paint in the stitching along the clothing seam lines and fabric print detail on the shirt, pants and patches. Use the photos for detailed painting ideas.

8. Once the detail painting is finished, completely seal the cutout by painting two protective coats of exterior polyurethane to all surfaces and edges.

9. Complete the project by tying the following lengths of rope around the scarecrow's neck, waist, wrists and ankles:

(1) 36" for neck
(1) 48" for waist
(2) 24" for wrists
(2) 24" for ankles

Painting detail of the scarecrow's pants

Face Grid

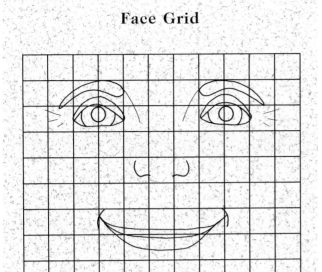

1 square = ½"

FIG. 21

Painting detail of the crow

Installation in the Garden

With a hacksaw, cut the 10-foot piece of conduit into two 5-foot pieces. Using the scarecrow as a guide, space the conduit pieces so they will be hidden behind her legs and drive the pipes into the ground. Attach the scarecrow to the conduit pipes with four pipe straps and eight ¾" × #6 galvanized wood screws (for further details see Fig. 15 on page 36).

At summer's end, store the scarecrow in a garage or basement for the winter months. The following spring, apply an additional protective coat of polyurethane before setting her out in the garden.

HORSE-DRAWN WAGON

A fanciful yet functional horse-drawn wagon

If your child has been begging you for a pony, this just might be your answer. Children find this little brown bay irresistible, and he comes complete with a harness. The wagon he pulls is a perfect planter box for flowers and vegetables. Once the growing season is over, use this team for an outdoor autumn display (see page 144).

MATERIALS LIST

Wagon

A – posts	3½" × 3½" × 36"	(4)	treated 4×4
B – floor supports	1½" × 3½" × 55½"	(2)	cedar 2×4
C – floor boards	1½" × 3½" × 30"	(12)	cedar 2×4
D – floor boards	1½" × 3½" × 23"	(2)	cedar 2×4
E – side boards	¾" × 5½" × 57"	(4)	cedar 1×6
F – side boards	¾" × 3" × 57"	(2)	cedar 1×4
G – side boards	¾" × 5½" × 30"	(4)	cedar 1×6
H – side boards	¾" × 3" × 30"	(2)	cedar 1×4
I – side braces	1½" × 1½" × 7½"	(6)	cedar 2×2
J – side rails	1½" × 1½" × 60"	(2)	cedar 2×2
K – end rails	1½" × 1½" × 34½"	(2)	cedar 2×2
L – seat board	¾" × 5½" × 21"	(1)	cedar 1×6
M – seat board	¾" × 3½" × 21"	(1)	cedar 1×4
N – seat supports	¾" × 5½" × 10"	(2)	cedar 1×6
O – seat braces	1½" × 1½" × 5½"	(2)	cedar 2×2
P – wheels	¾" × 18" × 18"	(4)	¾" ACX plywood
Q – axle covers	¾" × 2½" × 2½"	(4)	¾" ACX plywood

2" × #8 deck screws	(50)
3" × #8 deck screws	(4)
3d galvanized box nails	
8d galvanized box nails	
12d galvanized box nails	
exterior primer/sealer	
exterior paint	

Horse

Horse	¾" × 44" × 48"	(1)	¾" ACX plywood
10' × ½" EMT thin-wall metal conduit		(1)	
½" conduit pipe straps		(4)	
¾" × #8 galvanized wood screws		(8)	
brass D-ring drawer pulls		(2)	
decorative brass drawer pull plate		(1)	
small brass cup hooks		(2)	
20' × ¼" black poly rope			
exterior primer/sealer			
acrylic craft paints (assorted colors)			
exterior brown paint			
exterior polyurethane			
carbon paper			

ASSEMBLY INSTRUCTIONS

Wheels

1. Enlarge the wheel grid pattern onto a piece of pattern paper; see Fig. 22. Once the pattern is complete, use scissors to carefully cut around the outline and the interior cut-out areas.

2. Next, lay the ¾-inch sheets of plywood across two sawhorses, sanded side up. Place and lightly tape the paper pattern to the plywood. With a pencil, draw around the outside and interior cut-out edges of the pattern piece, leaving a penciled outline on the wood. Remove the pattern and repeat the process until you have traced all four wheels onto the plywood pieces. With a compass, draw four 2½-inch circles on scraps of plywood for the axle covers.

3. Using a saber saw, cut the wood along the pen

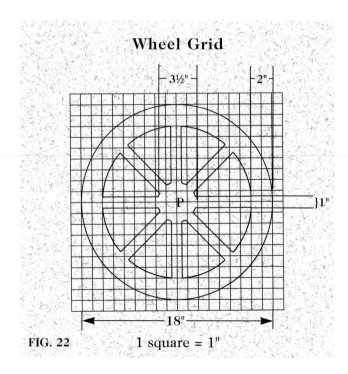

FIG. 22   1 square = 1"

cil lines. For the interior cut-out areas, drill ⅜-inch holes to allow access with the saw blade. Finish by sanding all surfaces and edges smooth.

4. Paint two coats of exterior primer to the front, back and edges of the wheels and axle covers. Let the primer dry completely between coats. Then apply two coats of exterior gray paint (you can use the wagon-gray). With an assortment of acrylic paints, streak on various shades of gray and light brown to make the wheels look as though they have been driven through mud. When the detail painting is finished, completely seal the axle covers and wheels by applying two coats of exterior polyurethane to all surfaces and edges.

Wagon

1. From the materials list, cut all the necessary lumber to size.

2. Begin the assembly by nailing one floor support (**B**) across two of the posts (**A**) using 12d galvanized box nails; see Fig. 23. The posts should be parallel to each other

and 24½ inches apart. The top edge of the support board sits 9 inches below the top of the two posts. The ends of the support board should extend 12 inches beyond both posts. Once nailed, this assembly will be in an "H" shape. Now repeat this step with the other support board and remaining two posts.

3. On level ground, stand up both post and support assemblies so that the posts are vertical and the support boards are horizontal. Place the two sections so that the support boards are on the insides of the posts and are facing one another. With the help of an assistant, nail the two floor boards (**D**) onto the floor support boards so that they span the two sections and butt up against the four posts; see Fig. 23. After you have nailed on the two floor boards, you will have defined the basic inner frame of the wagon.

4. Use this frame to locate the positions of the four post holes you will need to dig in order to anchor the wagon in the ground. Set the frame on the spot where the wagon will be permanently positioned. Mark the dirt around the four posts and lift the frame aside.

5. Dig four post holes, each one 13 inches deep.

6. Lift the frame up and set the four posts into the holes. Level the entire frame and make sure the posts are parallel to each other.

7. Fill in the loose dirt around the posts and tamp the ground firm.

8. Now you can complete the floor by nailing in the remaining floor boards (**C**) using 12d galvanized box nails. Leave approximately a ½-inch gap between each of the 14 floor boards. The two outermost floor

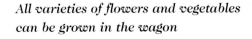

All varieties of flowers and vegetables can be grown in the wagon

Wagon Frame Detail

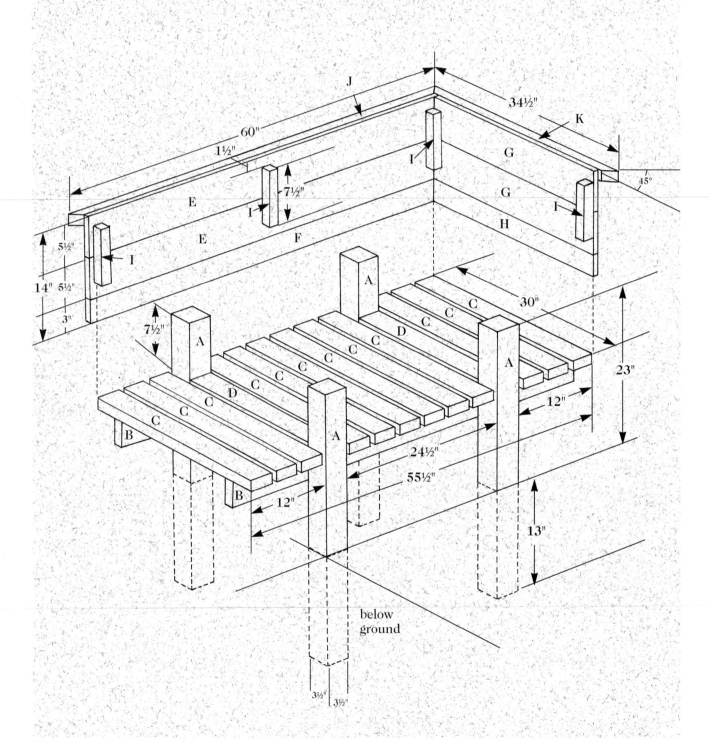

J

60"

1½"

7½"

34½"

K

G

G

I

I

E

H

E

F

I

5½"

14" 5½"

3"

7½"

A

A

A

A

C

C

C

D

C

C

C

C

C

C

D

C

C

B

C

C

D

C

B

30"

23"

12"

24½"

55½"

12"

13"

45°

below
ground

3½" 3½"

FIG. 23

Wagon

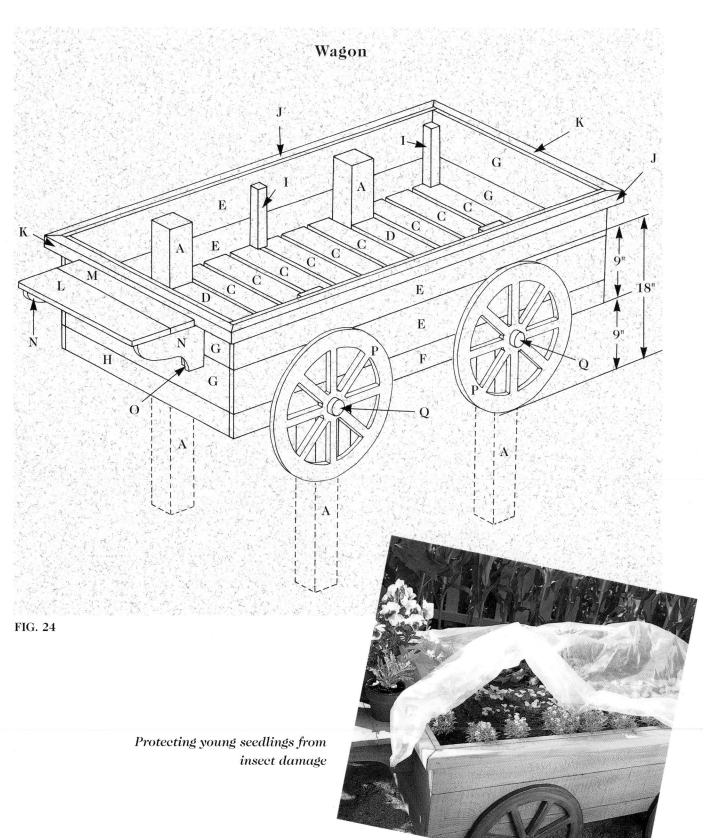

FIG. 24

Protecting young seedlings from insect damage

boards end up flush with the ends of the support boards; see Fig. 23.

9. Once the floor boards are nailed in place, you're ready to nail on the twelve side boards using 8d galvanized box nails. First, nail the two top boards (**E**) onto the posts, one on either side of the wagon. The top edges of these first two boards stand 1½ inches above the tops of the four posts. They also extend beyond the ends of the frame by ¾ inch on each side in order to match the edges of the end side boards. Complete the two sides by nailing on the remaining two boards (**E**) and the two boards (**F**); see Fig. 23.

10. Now complete the two ends by installing the end side boards (**G**) and (**H**). Attach them by nailing through the edges of side boards (**E**) and (**F**) and into the ends of boards (**G**) and (**H**) using 8d galvanized box nails.

11. Next, miter the four rail boards so they form a frame around the top edges of the wagon. Use four 2" × #8 deck screws on each of the long sides, and three 2" × #8 deck screws on each of the ends. Attach the rails from the inside of the wagon after pre-drilling the screw holes. Finally, pre-drill and install one 3" × #8 screw at each of the mitered corners to lock the frame together. Install these screws through the ends of side rails (**J**) and into rails (**K**).

12. The wagon box is secured further by a set of six braces (**I**). Position the braces as shown in Figs. 23 & 24. Anchor them to the 8 upper side boards using two 2" × #8 deck screws for each middle brace, and four 2" × #8 deck screws for each corner brace. Pre-drill and install the screws through the side boards and into the six braces.

13. Since the wagon is constructed of cedar and treated lumber, a protective coat of stain or paint is not essential, other than to give it the look of a real Old West wagon. If you decide to paint the wagon, first give it a good coat of primer/sealer. Finish off with two coats of exterior latex paint in a nice wagon-gray.

14. Now attach the four wagon wheels to the side of the wagon. Starting with your first wheel, drill a ⅛-inch hole through the center of the axle cover (**Q**) and the center of the wagon wheel (**P**). Install a 3" × #8 deck screw through both and into the center of one of the four posts (locate the center of the wheel at the bottom of the wagon box). Then drill a hole directly above the first hole in the middle of the outer rim. This time install a 2" × #8 deck screw through the wheel rim and into the post. The bottom edge of the wheel should just touch the ground. Repeat these steps with the remaining wheels.

15. To include the seat,* use the grid in Fig. 25 to make two seat supports. First attach the two seat supports (**N**) to the two seat braces (**O**) with two 2" × #8 deck screws for each brace; see Fig. 26.

16. Nail the two seat boards (**L**) and (**M**) onto the

The optional "seat" is a perfect place to set potted plants and tools

*__Important Note:__ The seat addition to the wagon is optional. The wagon seat is a fun and functional part of this project and gives the wagon an "authentic" look, especially when a willing horse is tacked up and ready out front. Unfortunately, this one is only designed to hold some potted plants or a few tools, not the weight of a child. Parents must, therefore, consider and decide whether installing the seat is appropriate for the family's use and enjoyment.

Seat Support Grid

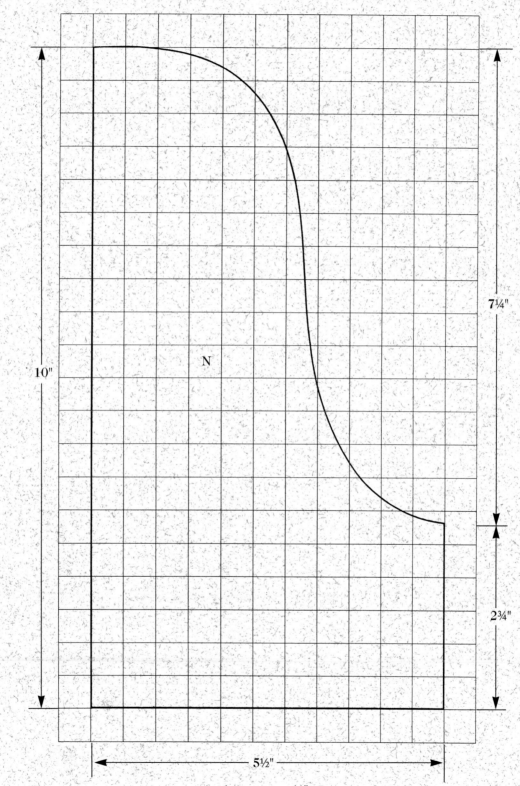

N

10"

7¼"

2¾"

5½"

FIG. 25

1 square = ½"

Seat Detail

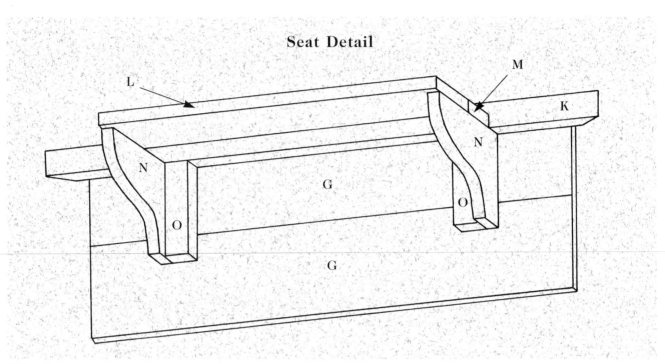

FIG. 26

top of the seat supports using 3d galvanized box nails (leave a 1½-inch space at the back of the supports where the seat slides in under the rail).

17. Attach the assembled seat to the wagon box by installing six 2" × #8 deck screws through the wagon box and into the seat supports and braces. As always, pre-drill the screw holes before driving in the screws. Use two screws to anchor each of the seat braces (**O**) and one screw to anchor each of the seat supports (**N**). Now paint the seat to match the wagon.

18. One last suggestion: First fill the wagon with a layer of small stones to help fill in the drainage gaps between the cedar floor boards. Then fill the wagon with a soil mix until it is about ½ inch above the tops of the posts. This will give you a soil depth of about 8 inches.

Horse

1. Enlarge the horse grid pattern onto a piece of pattern paper; see Fig. 27. Once the pattern is complete, use scissors to carefully cut around the outline of the horse.

2. Next, lay the ¾-inch plywood across two sawhorses, sanded side up. Place and lightly tape the paper pattern to the plywood. With a pencil, draw around the outside edges of the pattern

Hitched up and ready to go!

Horse Grid

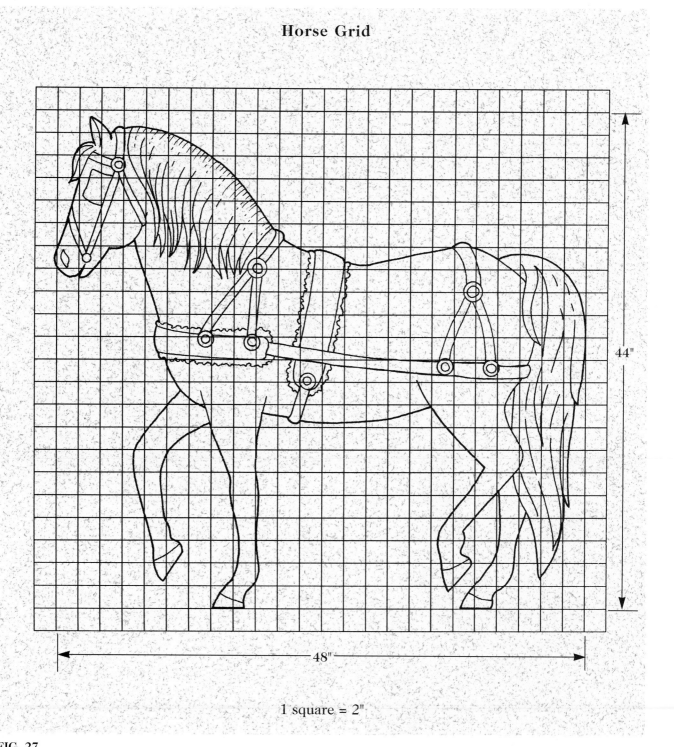

44"

48"

1 square = 2"

FIG. 27

piece, leaving a pencil outline on the wood. Remove the pattern from the wood.

3. Use a saber saw to cut the wood along the pencil lines. Finish by sanding all surfaces and edges smooth.

4. Paint one coat of exterior primer to the front, back and edges of the horse. Then apply two coats of exterior brown paint in the same manner. Once the paint is dry, re-tape the paper pattern piece to the cutout. Lifting the tape when necessary, slip a piece of carbon paper between the pattern and the cutout (carbon side facing the plywood). With a pencil, trace over the painting guide lines for the harness, mane and tail, facial features and hooves, leaving a carbon line drawing on the brown base-coat surface.

5. With your assortment of acrylic paint colors, paint on as much or as little detail as you wish. Use the photos for ideas.

Painting detail of the horse's tail

Painting detail of the horse's head and mane

6. Once the detail painting is finished, completely seal the cutout by applying two protective coats of exterior polyurethane to all surfaces and edges.

7. Finish the horse by attaching the decorative brass drawer pulls and plate that represent the horse's bit and D-ring on the girth. Drill appropriately sized holes at the corner of the horse's mouth and along the girth of the harness. Depending on the type of drawer pull, you may need to countersink and inset the screws on the back of the horse. Mount one D-ring at the corner of the mouth and the drawer pull plate and D-ring on the harness girth.

Painting detail of the harness

Installation in the Garden

With a hacksaw, cut the 10-foot piece of conduit into two 5-foot pieces. Using the horse as a guide, space the conduit so the pieces will be hidden behind the legs and drive the conduit pipes into the ground. Attach the horse to the conduit pipes with four pipe straps and eight ¾" × #6 galvanized wood screws (for further details see Fig. 15 on page 36).

At summer's end, store the horse in a garage or basement for the winter months. The following spring, apply an additional protective coat of polyurethane before setting it out in the garden.

8. At the corresponding points on the back of the horse, attach the small cup hooks which will hold the rein on the far side.

9. Make the reins by cutting the 20 feet of black poly rope in half and lightly singeing the ends with a match to keep them from fraying. Slip one end around the bit to form a loop, and lash it onto itself with fishing line or strong buttonhole thread. Slip the other end through the D-ring on the harness girth. Repeat the process to create the rein on the far side of the horse, slipping the rope over the cup hooks.

Every horse enjoys a treat now and then

COWBOY

This masked cowboy is always available to offer a helping hand

When this masked cowboy isn't holding up horse-drawn wagons, he's busy holding up your garden hose. Coiling hoses can be a tedious job for young gardeners, so they will appreciate this cowboy's helping hands. Standing four feet tall, the cowboy's outstretched arms are the perfect height for even the smallest hose-wrangling gardener. Held firmly with conduit pipes, the cowboy easily holds 25 feet of coiled hose. Happy trails!

MATERIALS LIST

A – cowboy	¾" × 12" × 52"	(1)	¾" ACX plywood
B – arms	¾" × 12" × 12"	(2)	¾" ACX plywood
C – arm support	¾" × 3½" × 12"	(1)	pine or fir 1×4

10' × ½" EMT thin wall metal conduit pipe	(1)
½" conduit pipe straps	(4)
¾" × #6 galvanized wood screws	(8)
1" × #6 galvanized wood screws	(3)
2" × #6 galvanized wood screws	(6)
exterior primer/sealer	
exterior polyurethane	
acrylic craft paints (assorted colors)	
brown exterior paint	
carbon paper	

Two hose-wrangling cowboys

ASSEMBLY INSTRUCTIONS

1. Begin by enlarging the grid patterns for the cowboy's body and arms onto two pieces of pattern paper; see Figs. 28 & 29. Make only one arm pattern, which can be flipped over to make the opposite arm. Include all the painting guidelines with the exception of his eyes and hands. Use the close-up grids of these features, Figs. 30 & 31, and trace them onto your enlarged paper patterns. Once the patterns are complete, use scissors to carefully cut around the outline of the cowboy and his arm.

2. Lay the sheets of ¾-inch plywood across two sawhorses, sanded side up. Place and lightly tape the two paper pattern cutouts to the plywood. With a pencil, draw around the outside edge of each pattern piece leaving a penciled outline on the wood. Flip the arm pattern over and again lightly tape and draw around the outside edge

Cowboy Grid

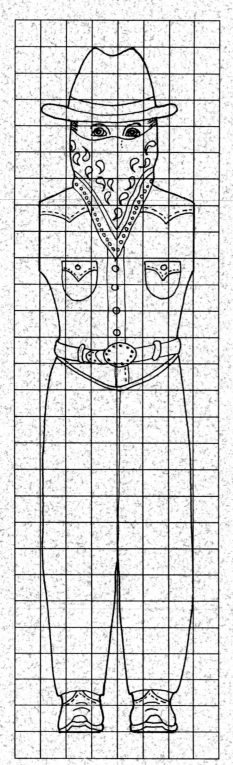

1 square = 2"

FIG. 28

Arm Grid

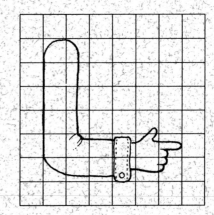

1 square = 2"

FIG. 29

Eyes Grid

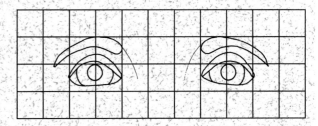

1 square = ½"

FIG. 30

Hand Grid

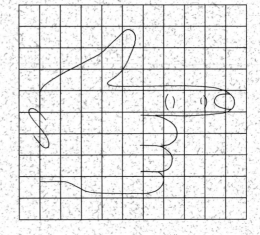

1 square = ½"

FIG. 31

Arm Support Board

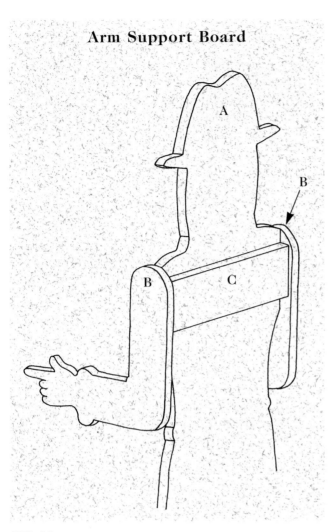

FIG. 32

to create his opposite arm. Remove the pattern pieces from the plywood.

3. With a saber saw, cut the plywood along the pencil lines. Finish by sanding all surfaces and edges smooth.

4. Attach the arm support board (**C**) to the back of the cowboy plywood cutout (**A**) using the three 1" × #6 galvanized wood screws; see Fig. 32. The screws are installed through the back arm support and into the plywood. Pre-drill and counter-sink the screws, spacing them evenly across the center of the support board.

5. Paint two coats of exterior primer to the front, back and edges of all the cutout pieces. Let the

primer dry completely between coats. Paint the back of the cowboy's body with two coats of brown exterior paint.

6. Re-tape the paper pattern pieces to the primed cutouts. Lifting the tape when necessary, slip a piece of carbon paper between the pattern piece and the plywood cutout (carbon side facing the plywood). With a pencil, trace over the painting guidelines leaving a carbon line drawing on the primed surface. Start by tracing over the large color-block areas such as the cowboy's pants, chaps, shirt, scarf, belt, face, hands, boots and hat (leaving off the fine detail items such as buttons, pockets, eyes, scarf fabric print and hat band until step 7). Remove the pattern pieces from the plywood cutouts.

7. Using your assortment of acrylic paints, paint in the large color-block areas. For example, use medium brown for his chaps, denim blue for the jeans, yellow for the shirt, red for the scarf and so on. As an optional detail, paint on any shadows or highlights at this time. For example, mix a small

Painting detail of the cow-boy's face

amount of black paint to the scarf-red paint and lightly blend-in shadows on his nose area and on the scarf. The shadows and highlights will add detail and a three-dimensional effect. Use the photos for ideas.

8. When these painted areas are dry, re-tape the paper pattern pieces to the cutouts. Once again, slip the carbon paper between the pattern and the cutout, this time tracing over the detail-painting guidelines (these include pockets, buttons, belt loops, boot detail, stitching around the seams, eyes, scarf fabric print, etc.). Remove the pattern pieces from the plywood cutouts. With your acrylic paint colors, paint in as much or as

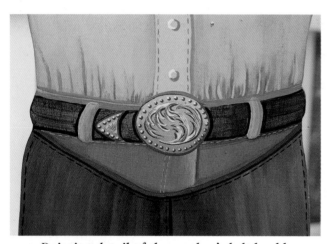

Painting detail of the cowboy's belt buckle

little detail as you wish. Use the photos for detailed painting ideas.

9. Once the detail painting is finished, completely seal the cutouts by painting two protective coats of exterior polyurethane to all surfaces and edges.

Painting detail of the cowboy's boots

10. Assemble the cowboy by attaching his arms (**B**) to his body using three 2" × #6 galvanized wood screws for each arm; see Fig. 32. Pre-drill and countersink each screw. Install two of the screws through the arm and into the arm-support board, install the third screw through the arm and into the plywood cutout. Place a dab of shirt-yellow paint over each screw head.

Installation in the Garden

With a hacksaw, cut the 10-foot piece of conduit into two 5-foot pieces. Using the cowboy as a guide, space the pieces of conduit so they will be hidden behind the figure's legs and drive the conduit pipes into the ground. Attach the cowboy to the conduit pipes with four pipe straps and eight ¾" × #6 galvanized wood screws (for further details see Fig. 15 on page 36).

At summer's end, store the cowboy in a garage or basement for the winter months. The following spring, apply an additional protective coat of polyurethane before setting him out in the garden.

COMPOST BIN

Compost in style with this classically designed bin

This elegant compost bin doesn't need to be relegated to the back corner of the garden. Its classic features make it attractive, while its sturdy construction provides years of service. Turning piles of debris into mounds of soil-enhancing humus is rewarding for you and your garden.

MATERIALS LIST

A – corner posts	4" × 4" × 72"	(4)	treated fence posts (true dimension 4×4)
B – corner finials		(4)	fence post finials
C – side rails	1½" × 3½" × 37½"	(4)	cedar 2×4
D – back rails	1½" × 3½" × 48"	(2)	cedar 2×4
E – front gate boards	¾" × 5½" × 39¾"	(6)	cedar 1×6
F – front gate guides	¾" × 1½" × 38"	(4)	cedar 1×2
G – back screen	36" × 46"	(1)	36", 2×4 mesh welded-wire fencing (25' roll)
H – side screens	36" × 34"	(2)	36", 2×4 mesh welded-wire fencing

10d galvanized box nails

8d galvanized box nails

fence staples

exterior primer/sealer, paint, or stain (optional)

ASSEMBLY INSTRUCTIONS

1. Begin this project by cutting the boards in the materials list to size. Use the grid to cut out the shape of the front gate boards (**E**); see Fig. 33. You will need four to six gate boards depending on how high you plan to fill the compost bin (note that the bottom gate board does not have an air-circulation notch cut from the bottom edge).

2. Cut the three wire fencing screens to size.

3. Next, dig four post holes 34 inches deep. Space them using the side and back rails as a guide; see

Working together to create rich, brown compost

Front Gate Board Grid

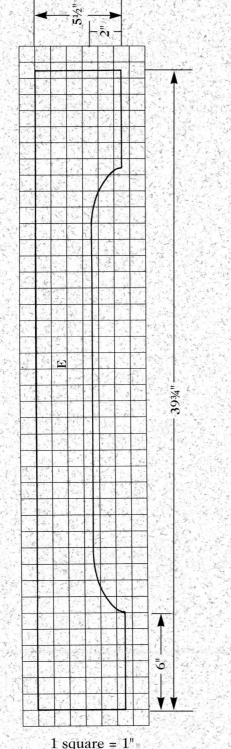

TOP

E

5½"

2"

39¾"

6"

1 square = 1"

FIG. 33

Fig. 34. Insert the four posts (**A**) and level their tops to each other. They should all stand 38 inches above the ground. During construction of the compost bin, tack scrap lumber across the tops of the posts to keep them plumb and true (once the side rails are in place these ties can be removed).

4. After the four posts are in position and tied together, fill in the loose dirt around the posts and tamp the ground firm.

5. Now install the three screens (**G**) (**H**) using wire staples to secure them to the outside edges of the posts. Each screen is set in from the vertical edges of the posts by 1 inch. They are also 1 inch below the top of the posts and 1 inch off the ground at the bottom. Try to keep the screens as taut as possible during stapling.

6. The two back rails (**D**) are nailed on next, using 10d galvanized box nails. The ends of these two rails are flush with the outside edges of the two back posts.

7. The four side rails (**C**) are nailed on next. These rails sit flush with the front edge of the front posts, and are even with the back edge of the back rails. Nail the side rails into the ends of the back rails as well as into the rear posts for added strength, then nail the front of the side rails into the front posts.

8. Now that the rails are nailed in place, finish stapling the fence screen to the inside edges of the side and back rails (both top and bottom). Each screen has now been securely fastened to the compost bin frame on all sides.

9. To complete the compost bin frame, nail on the four front gate board guides (**F**) using 8d galvanized box nails. True 4-inch dimension fence posts were chosen for this project so there would be a one-inch channel created between the two vertical guide boards. This allows the gate boards to easily slip into place; see Fig. 35. Remember that the bottom gate board is unnotched.

10. After all frame construction is finished, add a decorative touch by screwing on four wooden

Compost Bin

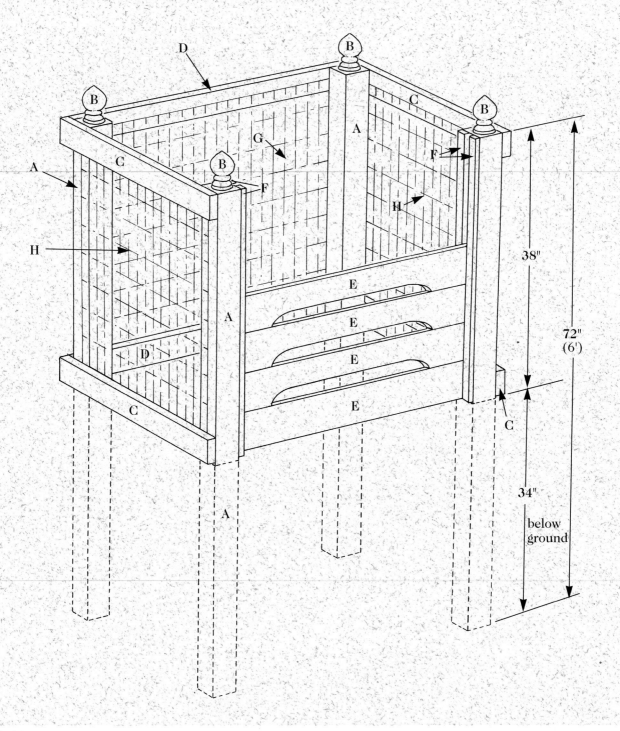

FIG. 34

fence post finials (**B**) on the top of each post. These finials are available at most lumberyards and come with a mounting screw in the bottom. Mark the center point on the top of each post and drill a ¼-inch hole in order to install the finial.

11. Since this project is constructed out of treated posts and cedar boards, a protective coating is not necessarily needed. However, if you wish to paint your compost bin, first apply a good primer/sealer to all wood surfaces.

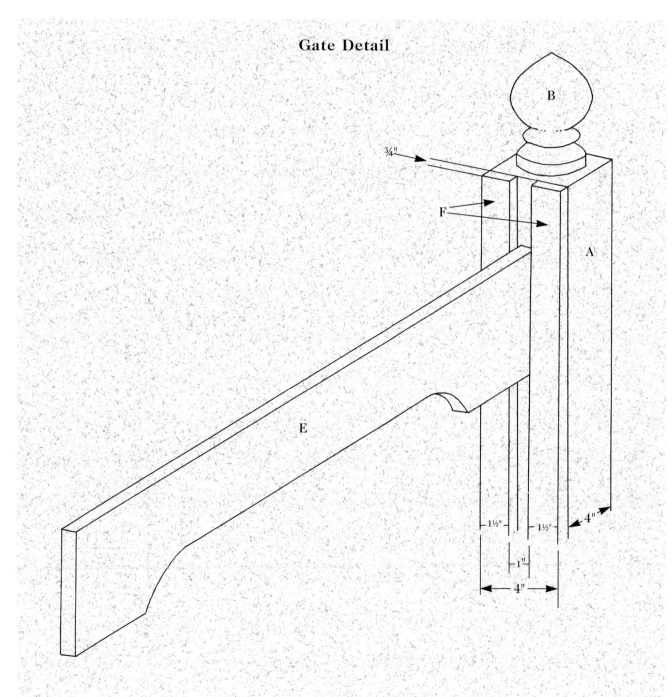

Gate Detail

FIG. 35

GARDEN SHED

A charming yet practical garden shed

This delightful shed keeps garden tools and supplies protected and organized. It teaches young gardeners the proper care of tools while also offering a place to hide during a rousing game of hide-and-go-seek. The shed's small size is perfect for any garden, yet large enough to be practical.

MATERIALS LIST

A – baseboards	1½" × 3½" × 48"	(2)	treated 2×4
B – baseboards	1½" × 3½" × 33"	(4)	treated 2×4
C – floor	¾" × 36" × 48"	(1)	¾" ACX plywood
D – front wall boards	1½" × 3½" × 81" [M]	(4)	standard 2×4
E – front wall board	1½" × 3½" × 41" [M]	(1)	standard 2×4
F – front wall board	1½" × 3½" × 24"	(1)	standard 2×4
G – front wall boards	1½" × 3½" × 8½"	(2)	standard 2×4
H – back wall boards	1½" × 3½" × 70⅛" [M]	(3)	standard 2×4
I – back wall board	1½" × 3½" × 41" [M]	(1)	standard 2×4
J – back wall board	1½" × 3½" × 41"	(1)	standard 2×4
K – side wall boards	1½" × 3½" × 81" [M]	(2)	standard 2×4
L – side wall boards	1½" × 3½" × 75¼" [M]	(2)	standard 2×4
M – side wall boards	1½" × 3½" × 69½" [M]	(2)	standard 2×4
N – side wall boards	1½" × 3½" × 38" [M]	(2)	standard 2×4
O – side wall boards	1½" × 3½" × 36"	(2)	standard 2×4
P – roof	¾" × 48" × 60"	(1)	¾" ACX plywood
Q – front siding	½" × 48" × 85"	(1)	½" sheet siding
R – right siding	½" × 36½" × 85" [M]	(1)	½" sheet siding
S – left siding	½" × 36½" × 85" [M]	(1)	½" sheet siding
T – back siding	½" × 48" × 72⅞"	(1)	½" sheet siding
U – door trim	¾" × 2½" × 68"	(2)	pine or fir 1×3
V – door trim	¾" × 2½" × 24"	(1)	pine or fir 1×3
W – rosettes	⅞" × 2½" × 2½"	(2)	purchased pre-made
X – molding blocks	⅞" × 2½" × 5"	(2)	purchased pre-made
Y – corner trim	¾" × 2½" × 85¼" [M]	(2)	pine or fir 1×3
Z – corner trim	¾" × 1½" × 85" [M]	(2)	pine or fir 1×2
AA – corner trim	¾" × 1½" × 73½" [M]	(2)	pine or fir 1×2
BB – corner trim	¾" × 1½" × 73" [M]	(2)	pine or fir 1×2

CC – door frame	1½" × 1½" × 68¾"	(2)	standard 2×2
DD – door frame	1½" × 1½" × 23½"	(2)	standard 2×2
EE – door frame	1½" × 1½" × 20½"	(1)	standard 2×2
FF – door panel	½" × 23⅞" × 72¾"	(1)	½" sheet siding
GG – handle plate	¾" × 2½" × 10"	(1)	pine or fir 1×3
HH – window frame	¾" × 1½" × 16" [M][R]	(2)	pine or fir 1×2
II – window frame	¾" × 1½" × 13" [M][R]	(2)	pine or fir 1×2
JJ – window frame	¼" × 1½" × 16" [M]	(2)	pine or fir lath
KK – window frame	¼" × 1½" × 13" [M]	(2)	pine or fir lath
LL – front roof trim	¾" × 9¼" × 60" [M]	(1)	pine or fir 1×10
MM – back roof trim	¾" × 9" × 60" [M]	(1)	pine or fir 1×10
NN – side roof trim	¾" × 9½" × 50" [M]	(2)	pine or fir 1×10
OO – finial block	1½" × 1½" × 9" [M]	(2)	standard 2×2
PP – finial block	1½" × 1½" × 9½" [M]	(2)	standard 2×2
QQ – finials		(4)	purchased pre-made

[M] indicates a board with one or more miter or angle cuts necessary. All measurements listed are pre-mitering.

[R] indicates a board with router or dado cuts necessary.

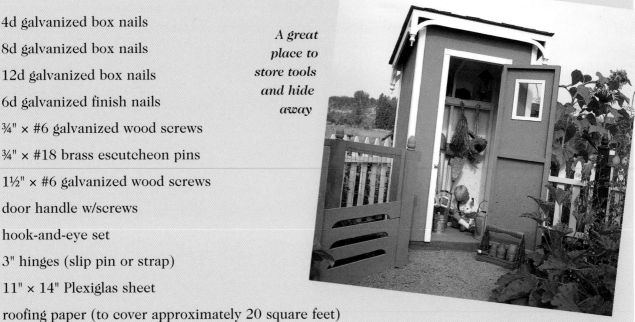

A great place to store tools and hide away

4d galvanized box nails

8d galvanized box nails

12d galvanized box nails

6d galvanized finish nails

¾" × #6 galvanized wood screws

¾" × #18 brass escutcheon pins

1½" × #6 galvanized wood screws

door handle w/screws

hook-and-eye set

3" hinges (slip pin or strap)

11" × 14" Plexiglas sheet

roofing paper (to cover approximately 20 square feet)

roofing (cedar shake or composition)

ASSEMBLY INSTRUCTIONS

1. Start this project by first cutting to size the lumber given in the materials list. The measurements indicated for all pieces containing mitered or angled cuts are the total lengths before mitering. After mitering, only one side of the piece will retain that measurement. Check all the appropriate figures and measurements to ensure your miters are correct. The roof has an 18-degree pitch; you will be using that angle (or its offsetting angle of 72 degrees) in all miter cuts except for the window frame boards.

2. Begin by nailing the shed base frame together using 12d galvanized box nails; see Fig. 36. Then, nail on the sheet of floor plywood (**C**) with the

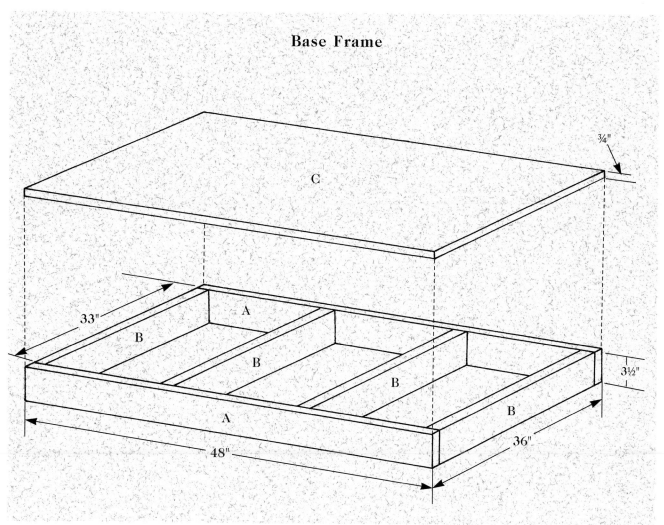

Base Frame

FIG. 36

sanded side up and using 8d galvanized box nails.

3. The four stud walls are constructed separately, then combined on the shed base; see Figs. 37–43. First nail each wall section to the shed base, then nail the four walls to each other along their adjacent sides. Make sure that all four walls are square and plumb before nailing.

4. Now attach the plywood roof sheet (**P**) using 8d galvanized box nails. Nail into the tops of the stud walls leaving 6 inches of overhang on each side and 5¼ inches of overhang on the front and back; see Fig. 43.

5. Trim to size the back siding panel (**T**) and nail in place using 8d galvanized box nails; see Fig. 44.

6. Trim to size the left and right siding panels (**R**) (**S**) and nail in place. Remember that the direction of the angle cut on the left side panel (**S**) will be the opposite of the right side panel (**R**); see Fig. 44.

7. Trim to size the outer dimensions of the front siding panel (**Q**). Next, cut out the door from the front panel. The door is cut out using a circular saw and a straightedge. Use a handsaw to finish the cuts at the top two corners of the door. The remaining opening should match the roughed-out door opening in the front stud wall. Set aside the door panel and nail in place the front siding panel; see Fig. 44.

8. All four siding panels are designed to extend ¼ inch below the plywood floor to help seal out the weather.

9. Now cut to size the door and corner trim pieces if you have not done so. Install the door trim pieces as shown in Fig. 44, using 6d galvanized finish nails. You may need to pre-drill the nail holes for the rosettes and molding blocks (**W**) (**X**) to prevent the wood from splitting.

10. Install the corner trim boards; see Fig. 44. These boards are all mitered to match the roof pitch, check the direction of each miter before cutting. Attach the trim boards with 6d galvanized finish nails.

11. Cut the window opening in the door panel (**FF**) using a saber saw; see Fig. 45.

12. Assemble the door frame as shown in Fig. 46, then nail the door panel (**FF**) to the door frame. The door panel is nailed flush to the frame along the hinge edge and the top edge. But it overhangs the frame on the handle edge and bottom edge. The overhang along the handle edge allows the door to open without scraping; on the bottom edge it helps keep the weather out.

13. The window is comprised of two frames. The outer frame is made from a routed length of 1×2; while the inner frame is made from a length of ¼-inch lath. Use the Fig. 47 diagrams to create the outside molding profile (cut the rabbet for the Plexiglas slightly full to help seat it more easily in the frame). Paint the inside edges of the window frame moldings now as the area will be inaccessible once the window is installed. After mitering the frame pieces to size, fit the four outside frame pieces in the window opening (**HH**) (**II**). Use small brass escutcheon pins to hold them in position. From the back of the door, install the piece of Plexiglas into the front frame. Line up the lath frame pieces (**JJ**) (**KK**) to match the inside edges of the front frame. Lock all frame pieces together by installing two, evenly spaced ¾" × #6 galvanized wood screws along the center line of each side.

14. Once the window is in place, mount the handle plate (**GG**) to the front of the door using two 1½" × #6 galvanized wood screws; see Fig. 45.

15. Then, mount the door to the shed frame with either strap hinges or 3-inch slip-pin hinges. If you use slip-pin hinges, recess the hinges before installing the door. Attach the door handle and latch (either a simple hook-and-eye set, or one of the many different types of latches that are available).

16. The next step is to install the roof trim pieces. Use the three grids to create patterns for tracing and cutting out the four trim boards; see Figs. 49–51. Note that the front roof trim piece (**LL**)

Front Frame

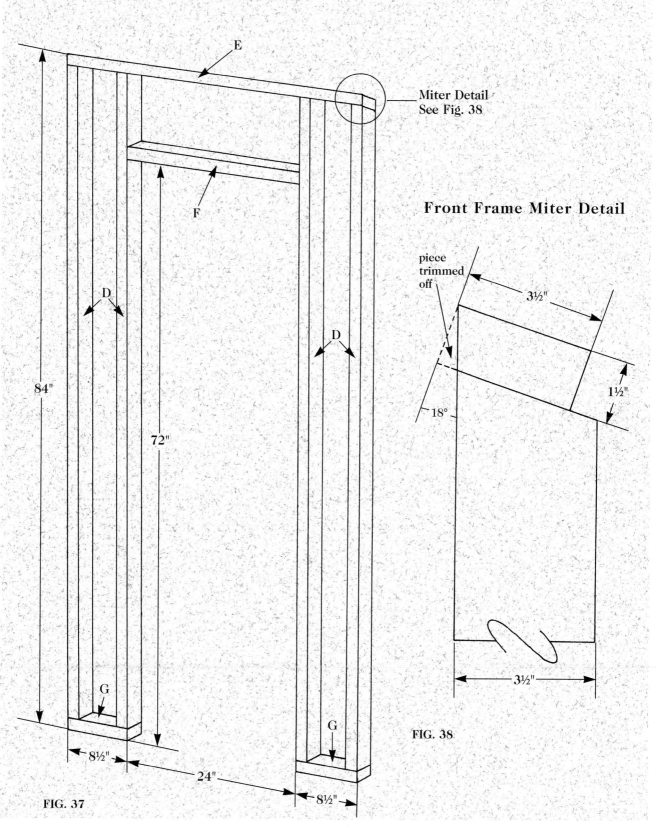

E

Miter Detail
See Fig. 38

Front Frame Miter Detail

piece
trimmed
off

3½"

1½"

18°

D

D

84"

72"

G

G

8½"

3½"

FIG. 38

24"

8½"

FIG. 37

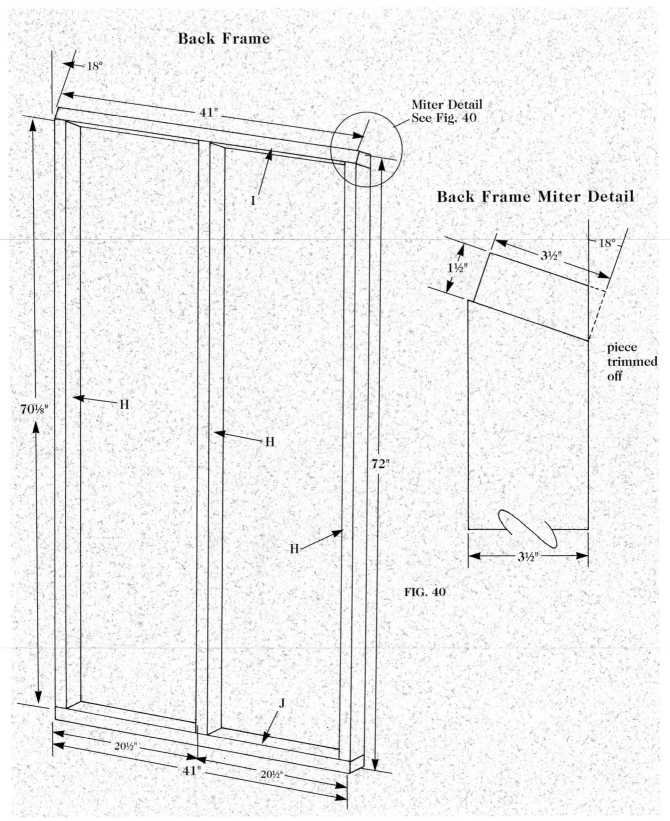

Back Frame

18°

41"

Miter Detail
See Fig. 40

I

70⅛"

H

H

H

72"

J

20½"

41"

20½"

FIG. 39

Back Frame Miter Detail

1½"

3½"

18°

piece
trimmed
off

3½"

FIG. 40

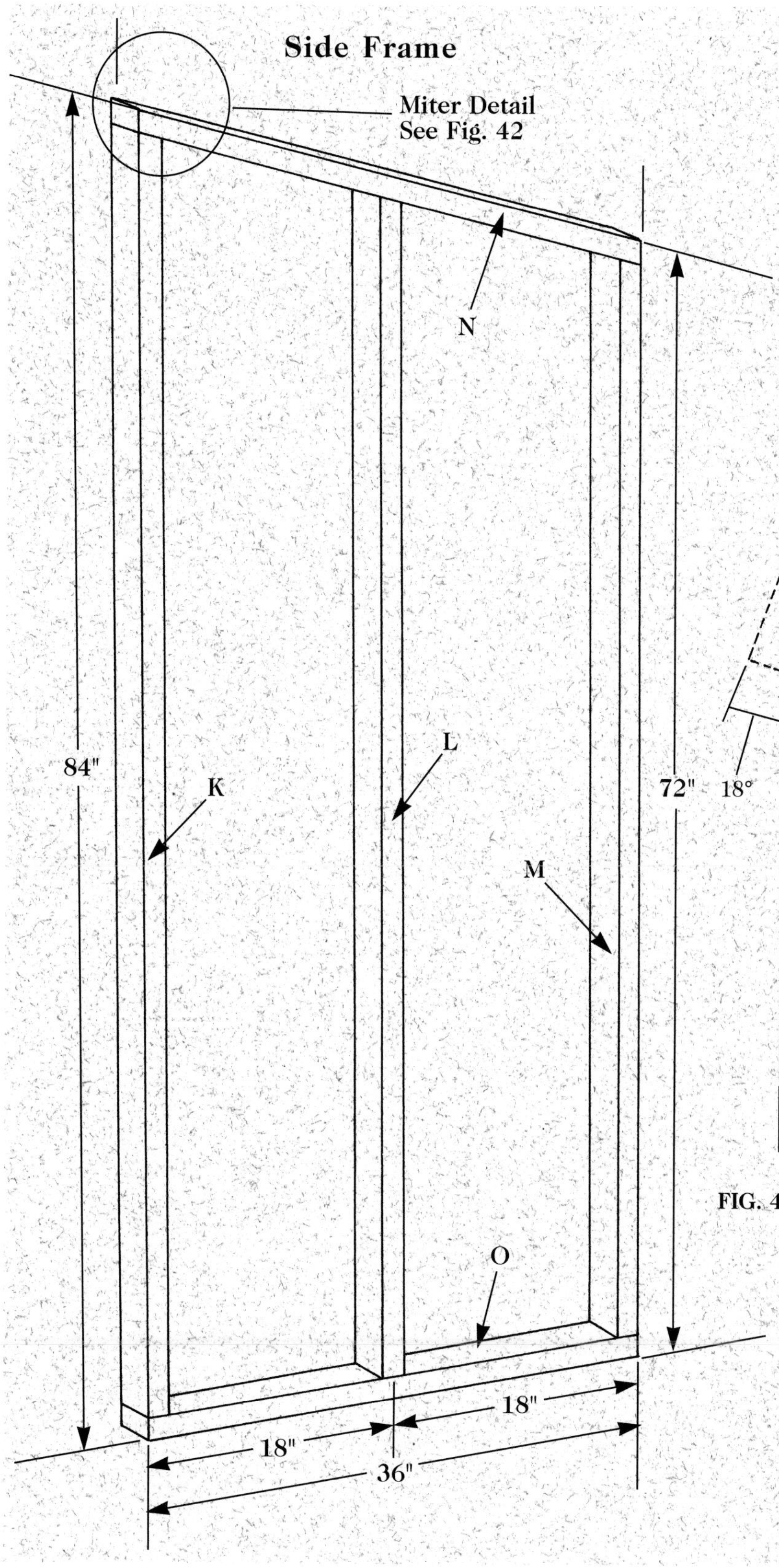

Side Frame

Miter Detail
See Fig. 42

N

84"

K

L

72"

M

O

18"

18"

36"

FIG. 41

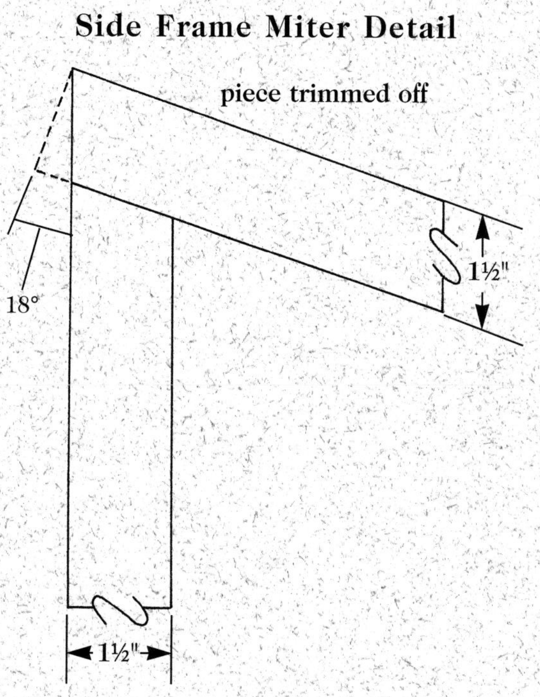

Side Frame Miter Detail

piece trimmed off

18°

1½"

1½"

FIG. 42

Complete Frame

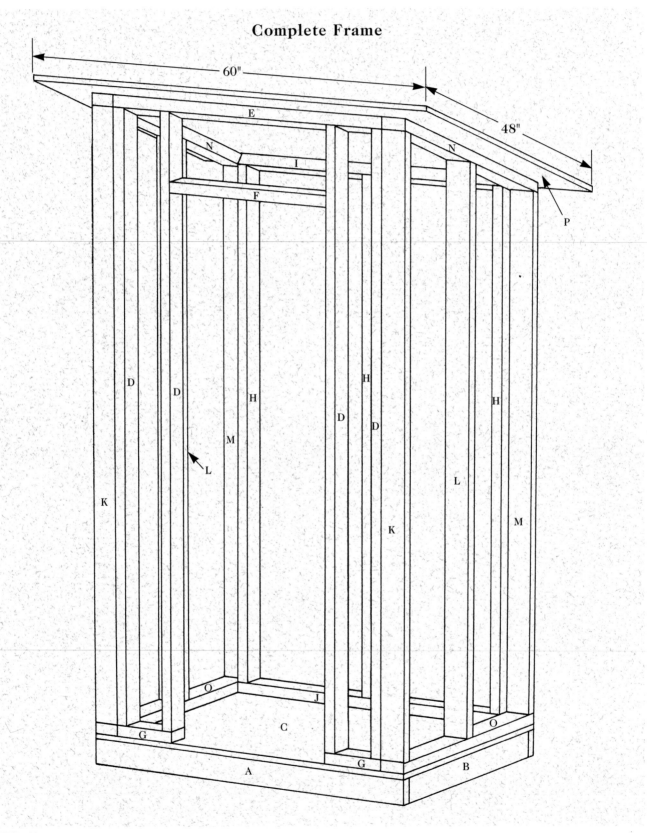

FIG. 43

Frame with Siding and Trim

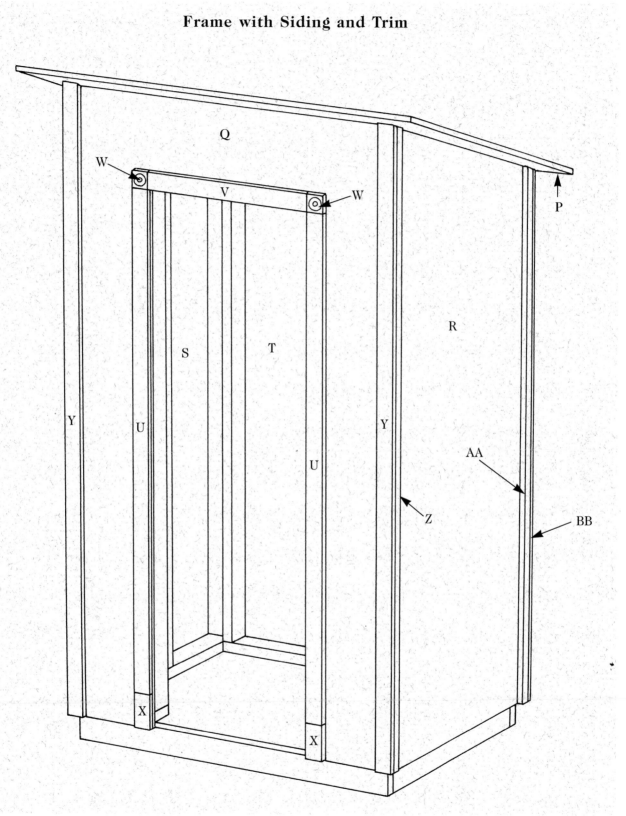

FIG. 44

Door Frame Front

Door Frame Back

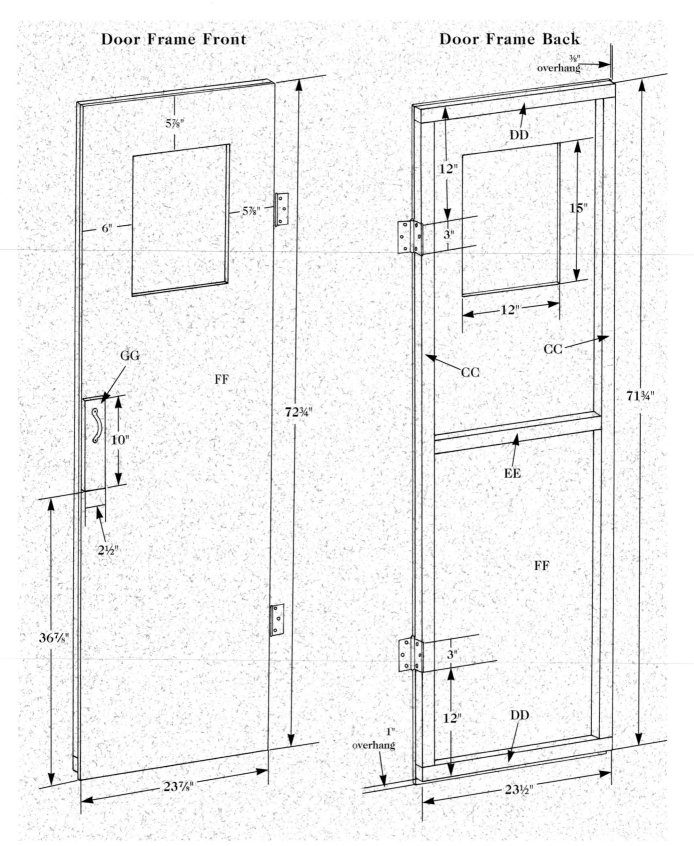

FIG. 45

FIG. 46

HH–II Window Molding Profile

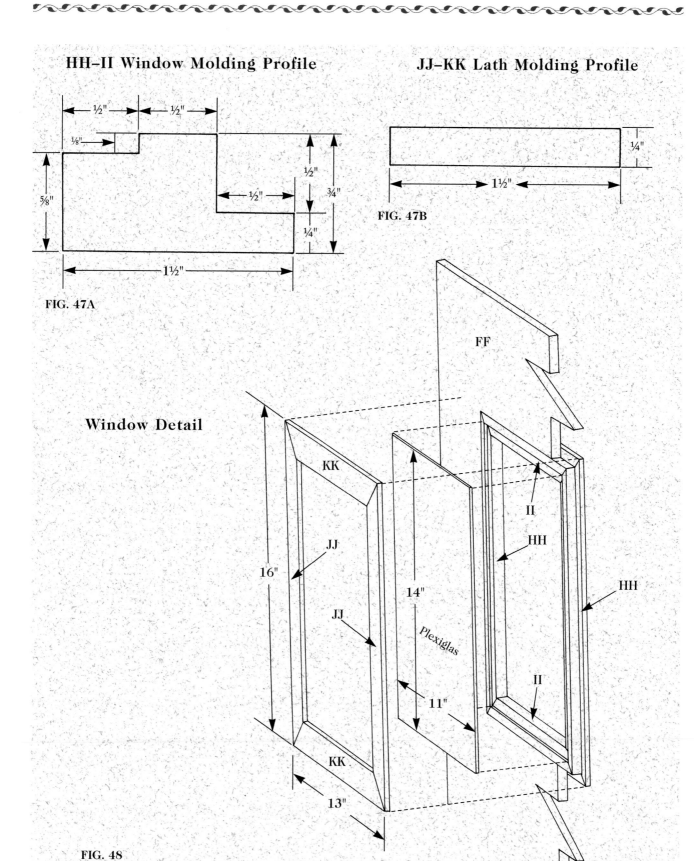

FIG. 47A

JJ–KK Lath Molding Profile

FIG. 47B

Window Detail

FIG. 48

and the back roof trim piece (**MM**) both have a mitered top edge; see Fig. 52. With the help of an assistant, attach the roof trim pieces as shown in Fig. 53. Use six 1½" × #6 galvanized wood screws to secure each trim board. Pre-drill from on top of the plywood roof (**P**) and install the screws through the roof and into the trim boards. Attach the front trim board (**LL**) first, then the two sides (**NN**), and finally the back (**MM**). Lock them together at the corners with 6d galvanized finish nails.

17. Install the four finial blocks (**OO**) (**PP**) on the inside corners of the roof trim by pre-drilling and nailing through the trim boards into the blocks; see Fig. 53. Again, pre-drill your holes to prevent the wood from splitting.

18. The finials are actually curtain rod ends that are available at most home and hardware stores. They come with a screw already embedded in the bottom. Center the four finials at the bottom corners of the roof trim; see Fig. 53. Screw them in place after drilling an appropriate size hole.

19. Complete the construction by stapling on roofing paper and your choice of roofing (cedar shake or composition shingles).

20. Prime all surfaces and finish with a good exterior paint; consider choosing a complementary color for the trim boards. And finally, apply a bead of silicone around the outside window frame, next to the Plexiglas, in order to seal out the weather.

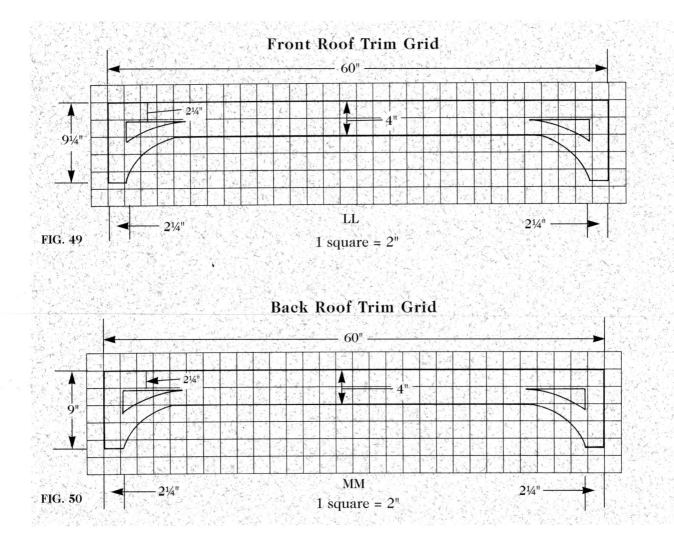

Front Roof Trim Grid

60"

2¼"

4"

9¼"

2¼"

LL

2¼"

FIG. 49

1 square = 2"

Back Roof Trim Grid

60"

2¼"

4"

9"

2¼"

MM

2¼"

FIG. 50

1 square = 2"

Side Roof Trim Grid

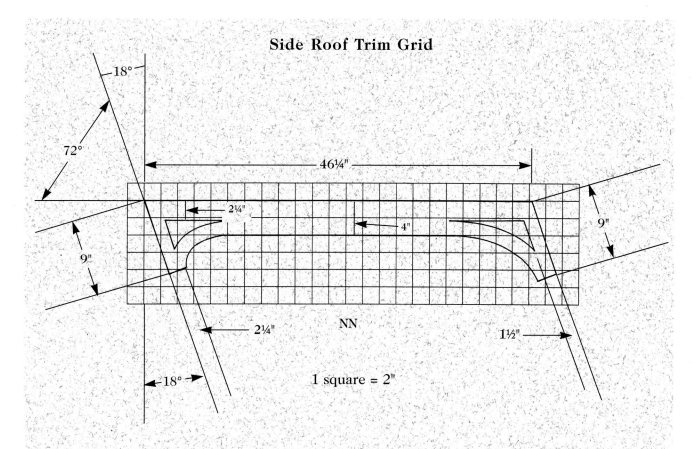

18°

72°

46¼"

2¼"

4"

9"

9"

NN

2¼"

1½"

18°

1 square = 2"

FIG. 51

Trim Miter Detail

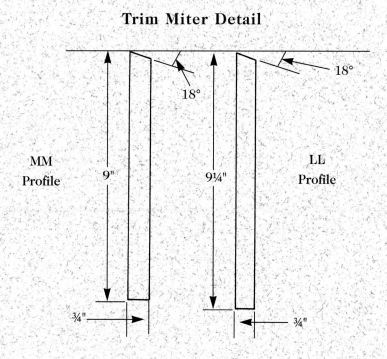

18°

18°

MM
Profile

9"

9¼"

LL
Profile

¾"

¾"

FIG. 52

Roof Trim

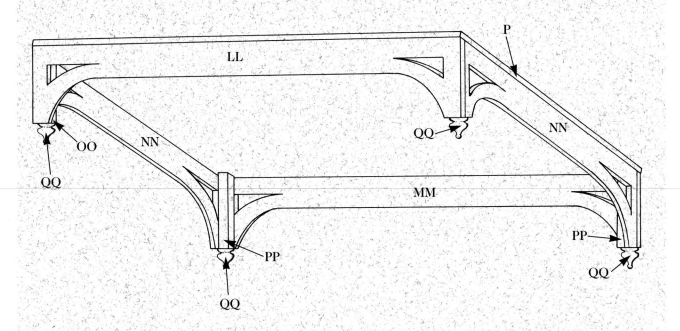

FIG. 53

TOPIARY

A topiary can be a whimsical addition to any garden

Large topiary standards are usually the result of a gardener's careful training and pruning over the course of several years. However, this easy to make ivy topiary will only take several hours to create. Adding charm and whimsy to any garden, this small tree will enchant both young and old.

MATERIALS LIST

4" ivy pots (with long vines)	(3)
12" half-round wire basket frames	(2)
13" clay pot (measurement refers to pot height)	(1)
small wire fence staples	(30)
42" straight, stout branch, approx. 1½" in diameter	(1)
46" slender young branches or whips, ¼" in diameter	(6)

(They must be freshly cut and pliable. Apple tree prunings or grapevines work well.)

72" of 21-gauge green florist wire

240" of 17-gauge wire cut into 8" lengths

moss

moss-green spray paint

potting soil

crushed driveway sand/gravel mix

ASSEMBLY INSTRUCTIONS

1. Begin assembling your topiary by attaching the slender whips to the stout branch; see Fig. 54. The whips give the illusion of ivy stems twining around the main supporting trunk. Attach one whip at a time by nailing it to the bottom of the main trunk with fence staples. Once it is securely nailed, gently wind it around the trunk (it may encircle the trunk only once). Use more wire staples to nail the whip at the top of the branch. Attach and wind the remaining five whips in the same manner.

2. Next, create the ivy ball frame with two half-round wire baskets; see photos on page 92.

3. Set the clay pot on smooth, level ground (once it is full of gravel the pot will be heavy, so consider assembling the topiary in the area where you intend it to stay for the summer). Have an assistant center the bottom of the main trunk over the inside bottom hole of the clay pot. While the assistant holds the trunk straight up and down, fill the pot to its rim with gravel; see photo on page 93. Water in the gravel so the rocks and sand settle around the trunk.

4. Lower the wire ball frame onto the trunk until the center of the top basket rests on the top end of the trunk; see Fig. 55. Nail the basket to the

Main Trunk

Trunk and Frame

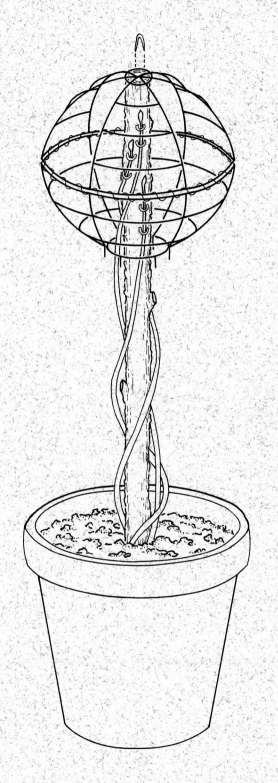

FIG. 54

FIG. 55

A 12-inch wire basket before cutting. You will need two baskets and a good pair of wire cutters to make an ivy ball frame.

Create the bottom basket by cutting out the very center where the wires are welded together. Bend the remaining wire prongs outwards at 90-degree angles to the basket. This will make a large opening so the basket can be easily slipped over the trunk.

Create the top basket by leaving the center circle and rim intact, but cutting out the remaining horizontal wires in every other section.

With the green florist wire, lash the basket frames together, rim to rim, to form the ball shape. Lightly spray the entire frame with moss-green paint.

The topiary pot being filled with gravel

extra security, push several greening pins into the moss to tack it in place. Conceal any other bare spots or wires by tucking in, or pinning on, extra pieces of moss.

8. Bend the 8-inch lengths of 17-gauge wire in half to create large greening pins (similar to big hairpins). Once the ball is mossy and green, wind the long ivy vines around the ball one at a time. Fix them in place with the greening pins. As the ivy grows, create a lush and leafy topiary by pinning down the new shoots rather than trimming them off.

Care Instructions

Like a hanging moss basket, your topiary will dry out quickly in hot weather, so daily watering may be necessary. Poke your finger down through the moss and into the soil to determine if the plant needs water. If it does, gently run water over the entire surface of the ball. The water will run through the ball and onto the gravel.

These topiaries make wonderful outdoor plants during the summer, however, if you live in areas of frost they will need to come indoors for the winter. Once inside, set the pot on a large plastic tray near a bright window. Water the topiary carefully because it will drain from the bottom of the ball. (Use a liquid fertilizer during the growing season.)

After one or two seasons the trunk may begin to rot and will need replacing. Start by making a new trunk. Then, remove the wire staples from the top wire frame, pry down the wire prongs on the bottom frame and slide the ivy ball off the old trunk. Remove the gravel from the pot, place the new trunk into the center and replace the gravel. Slide the ivy ball down over the new trunk and replace the wire fence staples. Finish by bending the wire prongs back in towards the trunk. Your newly restored topiary can live on for many seasons to come.

trunk end with one or two wire fence staples. Bend the wire prongs on the bottom basket back in towards the trunk.

5. Begin lining the wire frame with moss. Moss is easy to work with if you dampen it lightly with water. Working through the cut-out openings in the top basket, line the bottom basket with a single layer of moss. Firmly pack extra moss between the bottom wire frame opening and the trunk to keep the ball from rocking. Once the bottom basket is lined with moss, fill it to the rim with moist potting soil.

6. Next, line the top basket with moss and fill it with soil. Working through the cut-out openings, hold the moss against the wire frame while you add handfuls of moist potting soil. Press the soil up against the moss to keep it in place. Work your way up and around the top basket in this manner, leaving the three cut-out openings clear of moss and soil.

7. Remove the ivy from their pots and nestle one plant into each opening (roots facing the trunk with the crown of the stems even with the wire frame). Press small handfuls of soil around the root balls until the three openings are firmly packed with soil. Place a sheet of moss over each opening, working it around the crown of each ivy plant, and tucking the edges under the wires. For

ROW MARKERS

Reusable, laminated row markers

No garden would be complete without row markers. They designate where each specific flower and vegetable is located in a newly seeded bed. If you grow favorite varieties year after year, you will like these durable, reusable, waterproof markers. The plastic lamination preserves the face of the seed packet while the decorative border adds charm to the garden bed. The markers are large and colorful, making them fun and easy for young gardeners to handle.

MATERIALS LIST
(needed to make one row marker)

wooden stake (pointed at one end)	¾" × 1½" × 18"	(1)	cedar 1×2
¾" × #18 brass escutcheon pins		(2)	

exterior primer/sealer

exterior enamel paint

glue

empty seed packet

use of color photocopier (at most photocopy shops)

use of plastic laminator (at most photocopy shops)

ASSEMBLY INSTRUCTIONS

1. First decide how many row markers you want to make. Then take this book to your local photocopy shop and have them reproduce the illustrated row marker border on their color photocopy machine.

2. Decide which seed packets will be featured on your row markers and then carefully cut the front face off of each chosen packet (make sure to include the name of the plant). Next, following the outline, use scissors to cut out the photocopied borders.

3. Glue each seed packet front to the blank center square of each photocopy border.

4. Return to the copy shop and have them run the markers through a plastic laminating machine. With scissors, trim off the excess laminated plastic approximately ½ inch from the paper border.

5. Paint the wooden stakes with one coat of exte-

*Children
like these row markers
because of their bright colors and large size*

rior primer and two coats of enamel paint. Once the paint has dried, carefully nail each laminated marker to a stake. Make sure you drive the nails through the plastic lamination only; piercing through any part of the paper border would allow moisture to enter the inside of the marker.

6. As you sow your flower and vegetable seeds,

mark the end of each row with the appropriate marker. Once the seeds have germinated, remove the markers from the garden and store them indoors. This will prevent them from fading and preserve the paint so they can be utilized and enjoyed through several more seasons.

6½"

5⅝"

Make color photocopies of this border

PLANT CADDY

The plant caddy being used as a garden tote

Hand tools; seed packets, balls of twine, row markers—everyone can use some help toting supplies to and from the garden. This charming carrot-topped plant caddy is the answer and it will be enjoyed and utilized by every member of the family. Once the garden is finished, the caddy can also serve as a decorative potted plant holder.

MATERIALS LIST

A – carrot leaves	¼" × 9" × 12"	(2)	sanded plywood
B – carrot handle	¾" × 2½" × 15¾"	(1)	poplar (or similar)
C – side walls	¾" × 2½" × 15¾"	(2)	poplar (or similar)
D – end walls	¾" × 2½" × 9½"	(2)	poplar (or similar)
E – floor pieces	¼" × 3½" × 15¾"	(3)	poplar (or similar)

¾" × #8 brass wood screws

4d galvanized finish nails

3d galvanized box nails

wood filler

The plant caddy being used as a potted plant holder

ASSEMBLY INSTRUCTIONS

Caddy Box

1. To make the plant caddy, begin by making the caddy box. Cut to size the wall and floor pieces as given in the materials list.

2. Nail the two side walls (**C**) to the ends of the two end walls (**D**) using two 4d galvanized finish nails at each joint; see Fig. 56. Pre-drill the nail holes using a ¹⁄₁₆-inch drill bit. Countersink and fill the holes.

3. Next install the three floor pieces (**E**) to the bottom of the caddy box. Leave a ¼-inch gap between the middle and outside floor pieces. Before nailing, pre-drill the nail holes using a ¹⁄₁₆-inch drill bit. Use three 3d galvanized box nails to secure the ends of each floor piece and six nails along the two sides of the box.

4. Sand the entire caddy box smooth before applying a coat of primer/sealer. Once the primer is completely dry you can paint on your final coat of exterior paint in a color matching the carrots or leaves.

5. Set the caddy box aside and work on the carrot handle.

Carrot Handle

1. Enlarge the grid patterns for the carrot handle and leaf supports onto two separate pieces of pattern paper; see Figs. 57 & 58. Include all the painting guidelines. Once the patterns are complete, use scissors to carefully cut around the

Caddy Box

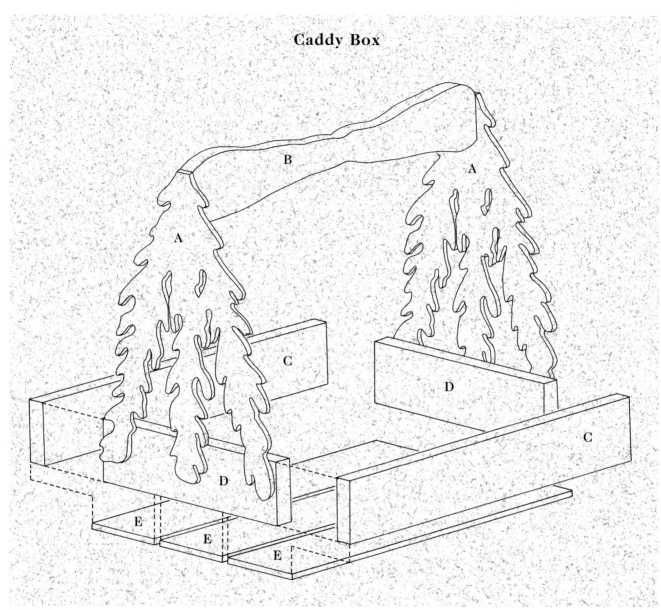

FIG. 56

Carrot Handle Grid

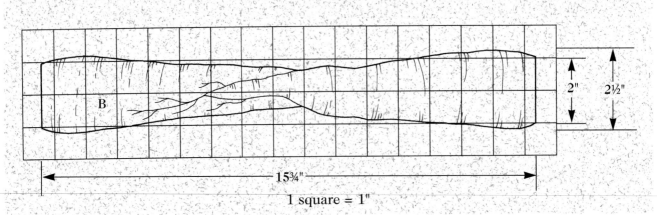

2"

2½"

15¾"

1 square = 1"

FIG. 57

Carrot Leaves Grid

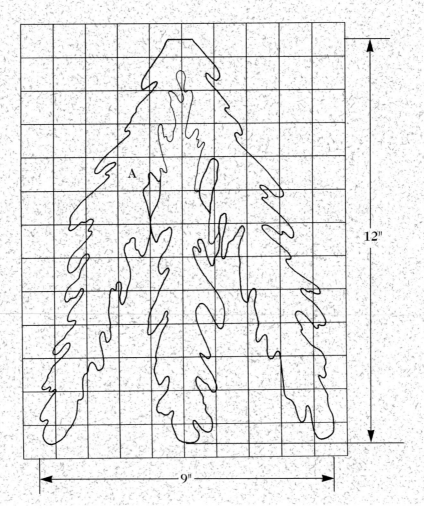

1 square = 1"

12"

9"

FIG. 58

outline and the interior cut-out areas of the paper pattern pieces.

2. Tape the carrot pattern to the carrot handle board (**B**). With a pencil, draw around the outside edge of the pattern piece leaving a penciled outline on the wood. Remove the pattern piece.

3. With a saber saw, cut the wood along the penciled outline. Finish by sanding all the surfaces and edges smooth.

4. Tape the leaf pattern to the first of the two plywood panels (**A**). With a pencil draw around the outside edge and the edges of the interior cut-out areas, leaving a penciled outline on the plywood. Flip the pattern over and re-tape it to the other panel (**A**) and trace out another leaf support. Remove the pattern piece from the wood.

5. With a jigsaw or coping saw, carefully cut out the leaves. Drill a ¼-inch hole in the center of each cut-out area to allow access with the saw blade. Finish by sanding all the surfaces and edges smooth.

6. Paint two coats of exterior primer/sealer to the front, back and edges of the cutouts. Let the primer dry completely between coats.

7. Use your acrylic paints to apply a base coat of green on the leaves and orange on the carrots. Do any shading to the carrots and leaves at this time.

8. Once the paint is dry, re-tape the pattern pieces to the cutouts. Slip a piece of carbon paper between the pattern piece and the cutout (carbon side facing the wood). With a pencil, trace over the painting guidelines, leaving a carbon-line drawing on the base coat surface. Remove the patterns.

9. Finish painting in the details of the feathery leaves and carrot roots. Use the photos for detailed painting ideas.

10. Attach the two carrot leaves to the carrot handle using two ¾" × #8 brass wood screws. Countersink the holes so that the screw heads are

Painting detail of the carrot handle

Painting detail of the carrot leaves

flush to the surface of the leaves; see Fig. 56. Apply a dab of green paint to all four screw heads.

Combining the Caddy Box and Handle

1. The final step in this project attaches the carrot handle to the caddy box. At the end of each carrot leaf, drill a ⅛-inch hole about ½ inch from the bottom of each leaf (six holes total).

2. Next, countersink these holes so the six brass screw heads will sit flush to the plywood leaf surface. Position the bottom of the carrot leaves approximately 1 inch from the bottom of the caddy box; see Fig. 59. Make sure that the leaves sit perpendicular to the base. After installing all six screws, touch up the screw heads with a dab of green paint.

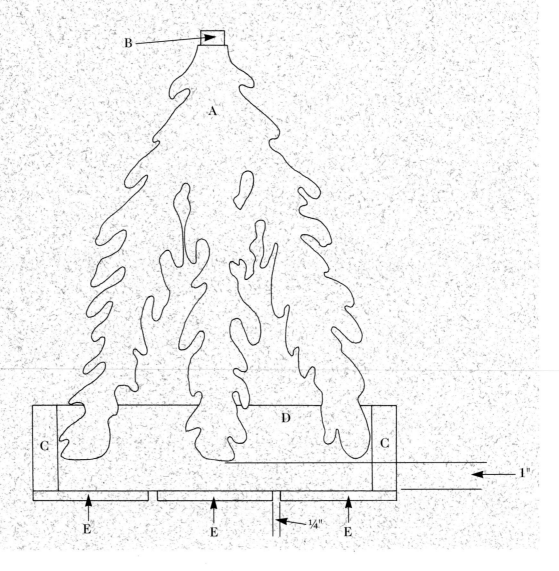

Carrot Leaves End View

FIG. 59

VEGETABLE TRELLIS

This trellis, with a mural header board depicting stylized root crops, is both fun and functional

To conserve valuable ground space, vine vegetables such as cucumbers can be grown on trellises. In the case of tomatoes and peas, staking and trellising is essential. This easy-to-make vegetable trellis is a wonderful aid to growing these varieties in small areas. Its mural header board depicts a cross section of soil in a vegetable garden. The brightly rendered root crops let children have a sneak-peek at what's growing beneath the soil's surface.

MATERIALS LIST

Trellis Frame

A – end posts	4" × 4" × 84"	(2)	treated fence posts (true dimension 4×4)
B – spanner rails	1½" × 3½" × 86"	(2)	standard 2×4
C – side rails	1½" × 1½" × 33"	(2)	standard 2×2
D – fence post caps	¾" × 5" × 5"	(2)	purchased pre-made
E – fence post finials		(2)	purchased pre-made
F – fence rail hangers		(4)	galvanized hanger
G – fence screen	36" × 84"	(1)	36" wide, 2×4 mesh welded-wire fencing

8d galvanized box nails

4d galvanized box nails

exterior primer/sealer

exterior paint

Header Board

H – header board	¾" × 11½" × 86"	(1)	pine

exterior primer/sealer

exterior polyurethane

acrylic craft paints (assorted colors)

1½" × #8 exterior deck screws   (3)

carbon paper

ASSEMBLY INSTRUCTIONS

Vegetable Trellis Frame

1. The vegetable trellis frame is relatively easy to build. Begin by cutting the lumber to size as given in the materials list.

2. Use one of the spanner rails (**B**) to mark the location of the post holes for the two end posts (**A**). At these points, dig two post holes 36 inches deep. Before inserting the posts in the ground, mark the location of the fence hangers (**F**) on the inside edges of the two posts; see Fig. 60. The bottom edges of the top fence hangers are 7½ inches from the top of the posts, while the bottom edges of the bottom hangers are 44 inches down from the top of the posts.

3. Nail the hangers in place using 8d galvanized box nails and lower the posts into the holes.

4. Set the two spanner rails in the top and bottom fence hangers (don't nail them in place yet). Use the rails to properly space and level the two posts. Fill in the loose dirt around the posts and tamp the ground firm.

5. Permanently nail the spanner rails in place using 4d galvanized box nails; see Fig. 61.

6. Next, nail the two side rail pieces (**C**) with 8d galvanized box nails. The two pieces are nailed to the inside edge of the posts between the top and bottom spanner rails; see Fig. 60.

7. On the top of each post mark a center point and drill a ¼-inch hole about 2 inches deep. Now install the wooden fence post caps (**D**) and finials (**E**) (the fence post caps often come pre-drilled to accept the finial screws); see Fig. 61. Once the finial is screwed down tight it should hold the cap in place, however, you could secure the cap in position with a 4d galvanized finish nail.

8. Apply primer/sealer to the trellis frame before finishing with a good exterior paint. Choose a color that will match the painted header board.

9. Cut to length a section of 36-inch-wide, 2×4 welded-wire fencing. Attach this fencing (**G**) to the back side of the trellis frame with wire fencing staples; (the trellis frame is comprised of the two spanner rails (**B**) and the two side rails (**C**).

Mural Header Board

1. Begin by enlarging the grid pattern for the header board onto a large piece of pattern paper; see Fig. 62. Include all the painting guidelines and interior cut-out areas. Once the pattern is complete, use scissors to carefully cut around the outline of the paper pattern header board, including the interior cut-out areas.

2. Lay the pine board across two sawhorses. Place and lightly tape the paper pattern to the board. With a pencil, draw around the outside and interior edges of the pattern piece leaving a penciled outline on the wood. Remove the pattern piece form the board.

3. With a saber saw, cut the board along the pencil lines. In the center of each interior cut-out area, drill a ⅜-inch hole to allow access with the saw blade. Drill and countersink three screw holes 1½ inches above the bottom edge of the header board. Position one of the holes midpoint along the length of the board, and the other two approximately 1 foot in from each end. Finish by sanding all the surfaces and edges smooth.

4. Paint two coats of exterior primer to the front, back and edges of the cutout. Paint the back of the header board with the same exterior paint that was used on the trellis.

5. Re-tape the paper pattern piece to the front of the primed cutout. Lifting the tape when necessary, slip a piece of carbon paper between the pattern piece and the wood cutout (carbon side facing the wood). With a pencil, trace over the painting guidelines leaving a carbon line drawing

Trellis Frame

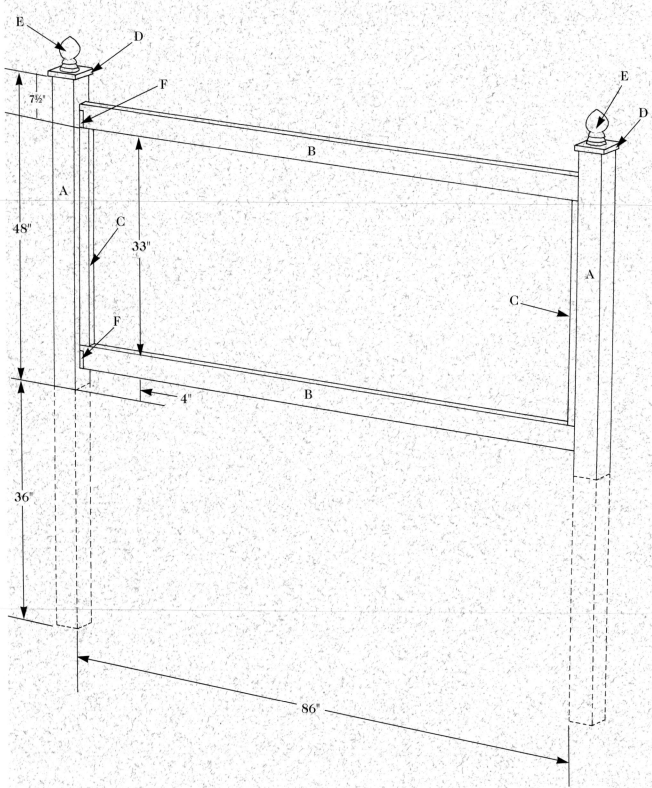

7½"

E
D
F
B
A
C
48"
33"
F
4"
B
36"
86"

E
D
A
C

FIG. 60

End Post Detail

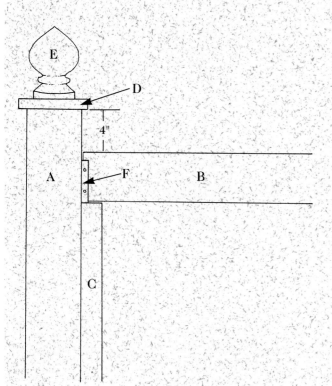

E

D

4"

A

F

B

C

FIG. 61

Header Board Grid

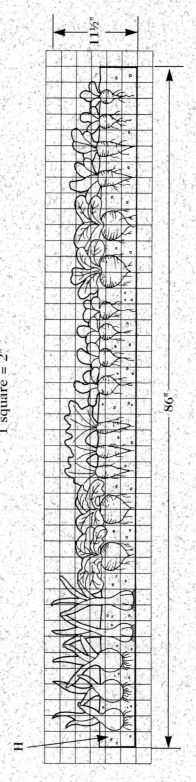

11½"

86"

TOP

1 square = 2"

H

FIG. 62

on the primed surface. Remove the pattern piece from the wooden cutout.

6. Using your assortment of acrylic paints, paint in the large color-block areas—for example, use medium brown for the soil, orange for the carrots, various greens for the leaves, etc. Once the base colors have been applied, add the details such as shadows and highlights, pebbles in the soil, roots, and veins on the leaves. These are stylized vegetables, so have fun and paint them in bright colors with freeform leaf shapes and maybe even add some worms to the soil!

7. Once the detail painting is finished, completely seal the header board by painting two protective coats of exterior polyurethane to all surfaces and edges.

8. Mount the finished header board (**H**) to the vegetable trellis frame with three 1½" × #8 exterior deck screws. Line up the bottom edge of

Painting detail of garlic

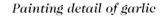

the header board even with the bottom edge of the top spanner rail; see Fig. 63. Then dab some of the soil-brown paint over the heads of the screws.

9. At the end of the summer, remove the header board and store it in a garage or basement for the winter months. In the spring, apply an additional protective coat of polyurethane before you reattach it to the trellis.

Painting detail of onions

Painting detail of rutabagas

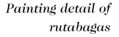

Painting detail of carrots

Painting detail of parsnips

Painting detail of beets

*Painting detail
of radishes*

Frame with Header Board

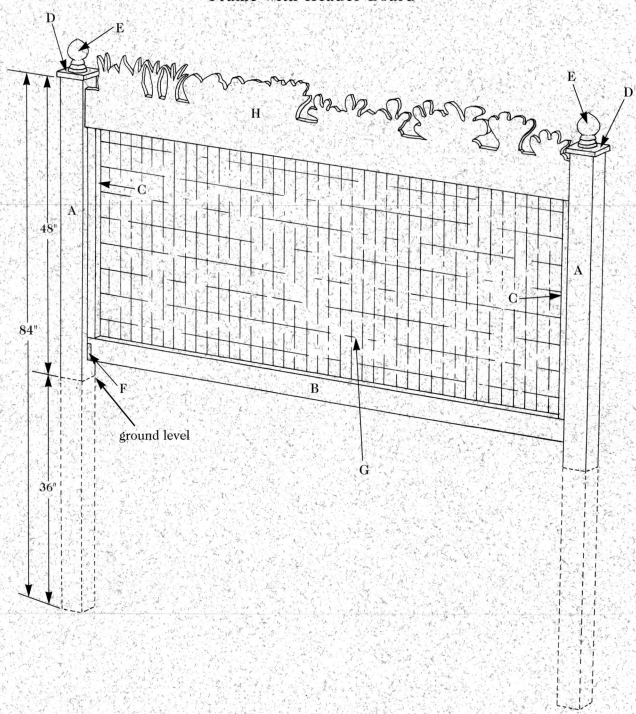

FIG. 63

SUNDIAL

The sundial in full bloom

Your children will know when it's lunch time, with a seven-foot sundial in the garden. The colorful rays, designating the hours, are created with alternating beds of purple and white alyssum. On sunny days, the pointer (or gnomon) casts a shadow across the flowers and hour numbers, making it easy to tell the time. With the numbers set at two-hour increments, the face of the dial displays the time between 6 a.m. and 6 p.m. This project is easy to construct and educational for young children who are learning their numbers and how to tell time.

MATERIALS LIST

4" wooden house numbers (see photo opposite; numbers are available at most hardware stores)	(2)	#1
	(2)	#2
	(1)	#4
	(2)	#6
	(1)	#8
	(1)	#0

A – gnomon	¾" × 5½" × 36"	(1)	cedar 1×6
B – baseboard	¾" × 5½" × 42"	(1)	cedar 1×6
C – doweling pins	¼" × 1"	(2)	purchased pre-made
D – hour rays	¼" × 4" × 41½"	(6)	cedar bender board
E – rim boards	¼" × 4" × 96"	(3)	cedar bender board
F – baseboard stakes	¾" × ¾" × 12"	(4)	cedar (scrap)

¼" × 16" wood doweling	(9)
small wire-fencing staples (or three small C-clamps)	(6)
exterior primer/sealer	
flat white exterior paint	
wood glue	
wood filler	

Plants	
Pink pansies	(8)
Yellow pansies	(8)
Dusty miller	(70)
Purple alyssum (1" plugs)	(80)
White alyssum (1" plugs)	(60)

ASSEMBLY INSTRUCTIONS

Numbers

1. Start by cutting the ¼-inch doweling into nine pieces each 16 inches long. Then, drill a ¼-inch hole, ½ inch deep, into the bottom of each number; carefully center the holes. Place a drop of wood glue in each hole and insert a length of doweling. Set them aside to dry.

2. Once the glue has dried, paint a coat of primer/sealer to all edges and surfaces of each number and dowel. Next, apply two coats of white exterior paint to all surfaces. Let the paint dry completely between coats.

Gnomon

1. Enlarge the gnomon grid pattern onto a piece of pattern paper; see Fig. 64. Once the pattern is complete, use scissors to carefully cut around the outline and the interior cut-out area.

2. Next, lay the cedar board across two sawhorses. Place and lightly tape the paper pattern to the board. With a pencil, draw around the outside and interior edges of the pattern piece leaving a penciled outline on the wood. Remove the pattern piece from the board.

3. With a saber saw, cut the board along the pencil lines. For the interior cut-out area, drill a ⅜-inch hole to allow access with the saw blade. Finish by sanding all surfaces and edges smooth.

4. From the remaining portion of cedar board, cut and sand a piece 42 inches in length. This is the base-

Sundial numbers ready for installation

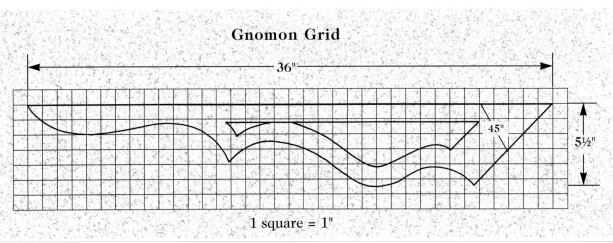

Gnomon Grid

36"

45°

5½"

1 square = 1"

FIG. 64

board (**B**) for the gnomon (**A**). Drill two ¼-inch holes, ¾ inch deep, evenly spaced along the edge of the board; see Fig. 65. Put several drops of wood glue into each hole and insert the ¼-inch doweling pins (**C**). Drill corresponding holes along the straight edge of the gnomon. Apply wood glue to these holes and along the straight edge. Fit the two cedar boards together, clamp them tightly, and allow the glue to dry. If necessary, use wood filler to conceal the seam.

5. Paint one coat of exterior primer/sealer to the front, back and edges of the gnomon and baseboard. Then apply two coats of white exterior paint in the same manner.

Installation in the Garden

1. Start by locating an appropriate and level site for your garden sundial. The area should be in full sun and clear of tree roots, rocks and sod. Pound a short length of pipe or conduit into the center of the area. Loosely tie a string around the pipe. Measure out 42 inches and tie a stake at this point. Keeping the string taut, walk in a circle around the center pipe, leaving a scored line in the soil. This is the outline of your 7-foot sundial. Leave the center pipe in place but remove the string.

2. With the line in the soil as your guide, use an edging shovel to cut a clean edge in the soil around the circumference of the circle. Then, with a shovel or spading fork, loosen all the soil in the interior of the circle (without disturbing the center pipe). Amend the soil with peat moss, compost and well-rotted manure. Mix it in thoroughly and rake the area smooth, preserving the clean edge around the circumference.

3. Once the soil has been prepared, use three 8-foot bender boards (**E**) to define the circle's outer edge. Gently bend each board around the circle, pressing them into the soil to a depth of approximately 3 inches. Their ends will overlap one another by several inches; see Fig. 66. As you work, it may be helpful to use small C-clamps to keep the boards from springing apart. One or two wire fence staples could also be used as temporary clips to hold the overlapping boards together. When all three boards are positioned into a perfect 7-foot circle, firmly pack the soil against both sides of the boards to hold them in place. It may be necessary to leave the clamps or clips in place for several days until the boards relax into their new curved position.

4. At noon on a sunny day, place the baseboard and gnomon into the sundial. Use the center pipe to position the base of the gnomon. Then, pivot the opposite end until the shadow cast by the

Baseboard and Gnomon

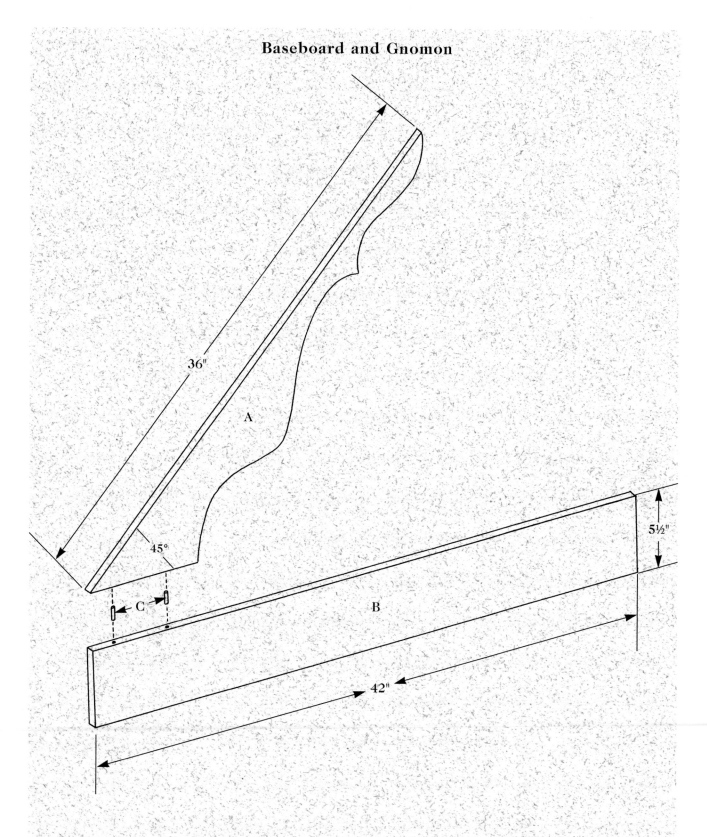

36"

A

45°

5½"

C

B

42"

FIG. 65

Sundial

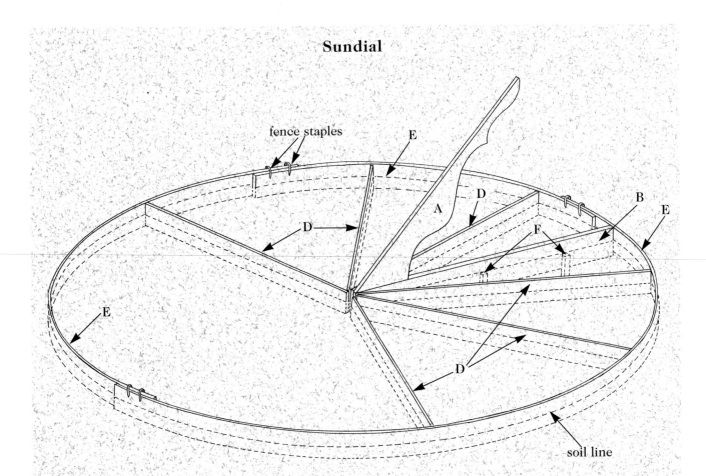

fence staples

E

D

A D B

E

F

E

D

soil line

FIG. 66

gnomon falls directly on the baseboard. Push the baseboard into the soil until the top of the board is flush with the perimeter bender boards. Remove the center stake. Secure the baseboard by tapping in two stakes (**F**) on either side of the board until they are even with the soil surface. Press the soil firmly around either side of the baseboard.

5. To create the rays (**D**) for the other hour designations, cut the remaining bender board into 6 lengths, each 41½ inches long. At 2:00 p.m. press one length into the soil along the gnomon's new shadow line, insert another along the next shadow line at 4:00 p.m., and another at 6:00 p.m. The following day (assuming you have sunshine!), repeat the process, starting at 6:00 a.m.; insert another at 8:00 a.m., and press the final ray in at 10:00 a.m. Gently tap the rays with a hammer until they are all level and flush with the perimeter bender boards; see Fig. 66.

6. Finish the installation by inserting the hour numbers just inside the rim of the sundial and beside their appropriate rays.

Planting Instructions

Your sundial can be planted with either flowers or vegetables as long as the plants are low-growing and compact. Alyssum, for example, is a perfect choice because it is compact, easy to grow and is covered in a carpet of blooms (see Sow Your Own Plug Flats on page 135). Other suitable flowers, under 7 or 8 inches tall, include compact and

On sunny days this timepiece is very accurate

dwarf varieties of lobelia, phlox, dianthus, marigolds and pansies. A medley of flowers and vegetables can be combined in the large area below the rays of the dial. Red and green leaf lettuce or colorful ornamental cabbages and kale would look dazzling surrounded by flowers. Use your imagination to create fun designs in wonderful color and texture combinations. For example, in the sundial pictured, the pale yellow and pink pansies add interest to the design and coordinate nicely with the white and lavender alyssum. The hard lines of the sundial rim are softened with a border of light gray dusty miller.

GARDEN BENCH

This bench makes a perfect place to rest or play

Throughout the summer every member of the family will use this decorative garden bench. It offers a seat to weary gardeners, a place to host a tea party or a peaceful venue from which to view and enjoy the garden. Morning glory vines wind their way up the trellised ends providing flowers, greenery and a bit of dappled shade. Whether you grow floral vines such as sweet peas or edible vines such as pole beans, this restful garden bench will always look charming.

MATERIALS LIST

A – side frame board   1½" × 3½" × 69½"   (4)   cedar 2×4

B – spanner board   1½" × 1½" × 16½"   (4)   cedar 2×2

C – spanner board   1½" × 1½" × 22½"   (2)   cedar 2×2

D – seat supports   1½" × 3½" × 22½"   (3)   cedar 2×4

E – seat boards   1½" × 3½" × 67½"   (6)   cedar 2×4

F – lower bench trim   ¾" × 5½" × 22½"   (2)   cedar 1×6

G – lower bench trim   ¾" × 5½" × 72"   (2)   cedar 1×6

H – upper bench trim   ¾" × 5½" × 22½"   (4)   cedar 1×6

I – upper bench trim   ¾" × 5½" × 72"   (2)   cedar 1×6

J – corner trim boards   ¾" × 5½" × 12"   (4)   cedar 1×6

K – end trim boards   ¾" × 5½" × 22½"   (2)   cedar 1×6

50' of 17-gauge fence wire

3d galvanized box nails

8d galvanized box nails

6d galvanized finish nails

8d galvanized finish nails

exterior primer/sealer

exterior paint

Tea time!

ASSEMBLY INSTRUCTIONS

1. Begin by cutting all the garden bench lumber to size, as given in the materials list. Use the three grids in Figs. 67, 68, & 69 to cut out the trim boards (**I**), (**J**) and (**K**).

2. Apply a primer/sealer and two coats of exterior paint to the bench pieces now rather than after the bench is assembled.

3. After each piece is painted and has had a chance to dry, begin assembling the garden bench by making the two end frames; see Figs. 70 & 71. Each end frame consists of two side frame boards (**A**), two spanner boards (**B**), one spanner board (**C**) and one seat support board (**D**). You will need to cut four notches in the side frame boards for the two spanner boards. Also, drill four ⅛-inch holes in each spanner board as shown in Fig. 70.

4. Now assemble the frame pieces. Toe-nail in the two spanner boards (**B**) with 8d galvanized finish nails. Nail on the top spanner board (**C**) with 8d galvanized box nails.

5. Thread the two 25-foot lengths of wire through the holes in the spanner boards as shown in Fig. 70. Once they are in place, hammer in two 3d galvanized box nails as shown and tie off two wire ends to each nail after pulling the wires taut (over time, as the wires start to sag a little, you can retighten them).

6. Once the trellis wires are secured, nail on the seat support board (**D**) 12 inches from the bottom of the frame; see Fig. 71. The seat support board is the same width as the frame.

7. Repeat the same steps to complete the second frame.

8. The next step is to connect the two frames with the six seat boards (**E**), which nail onto the seat support boards using 8d galvanized box nails; see Fig. 71. Evenly space them across the support boards leaving approximately ¼ inch between each board. The two outside boards end up flush with the edge of the frame.

9. Now install the third seat support board (**D**)

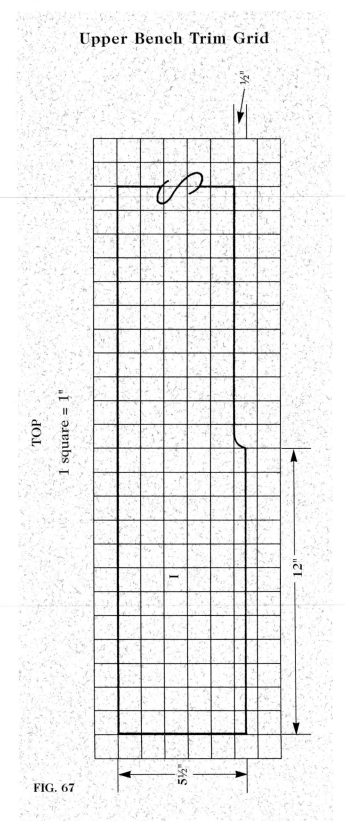

Upper Bench Trim Grid

TOP

1 square = 1"

½"

12"

5½"

I

FIG. 67

Corner Trim Boards Grid

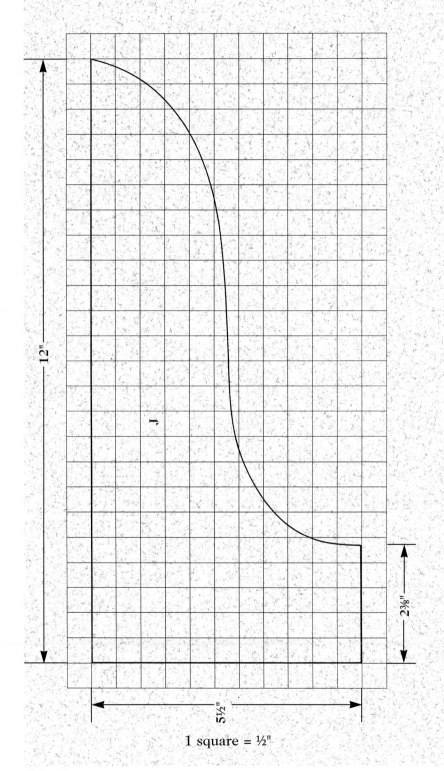

J

12"

5½"

2⅜"

1 square = ½"

FIG. 68

End Trim Grid

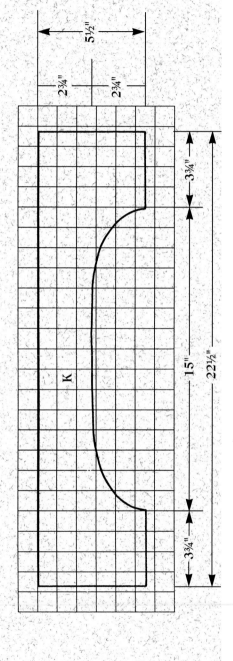

K

5½"

2¾"   2¾"

3¾"

15"

22½"

3¾"

1 square = 1"

FIG. 69

across the underside of the seat boards as shown. Nail through the seat boards using two 8d galvanized box nails per board. Shim or clamp the seat support board to the seat boards during nailing.

10. The garden bench is now ready to accept the final trim boards. Start by installing the lower trim boards (**G**) and (**F**); see Fig. 72. When in place, they should be even with the height of the seat boards. Make sure you drive one or two nails through the trim boards (**G**) and into the ends of each of the seat support boards (**D**). This will ensure that the middle part of the seat will not sag.

11. Next, nail on upper trim boards (**H**) using 8d galvanized box nails. These boards sit 1 inch above the top edges of the side frames to hide the tied-off ends of the trellis wires; see Fig. 72.

12. Then nail on the front and back upper trim boards (**I**) so that their top edges are flush with trim boards (**H**).

13. Now install the two end trim boards (**K**). They nail onto the end frame directly under the upper trim boards (**H**).

14. The final four pieces to install are the corner trim boards (**J**), located directly below the ends of trim boards (**I**). For each piece, nail in two 8d galvanized box nails at the wide end. At the narrow curved end, drill a 3/32-inch hole up through the tip and into the upper trim board (**I**). Then drive in one 8d galvanized finish nail to secure that end of the board. Repeat these steps with the remaining three corner trim boards.

15. Finish the bench by painting all the nail heads with a primer/sealer and two coats of exterior paint.

Installation in the Garden

Decide where you will locate your garden bench and then level the ground. Put the bench into position and do any further leveling. Loosen and amend the soil at either end of the bench and plant your twining vines.

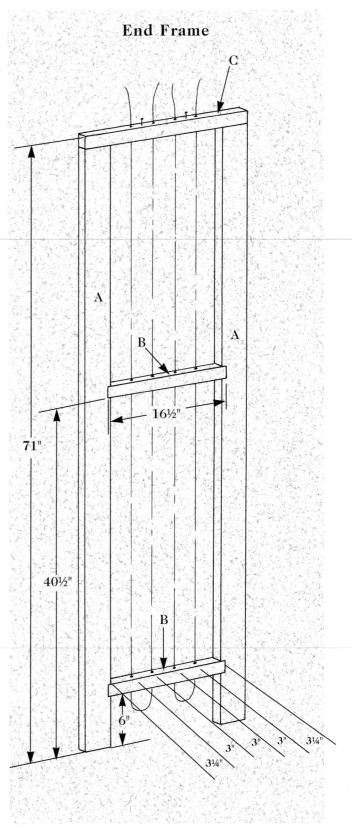

FIG. 70

End Frames with Seat Boards

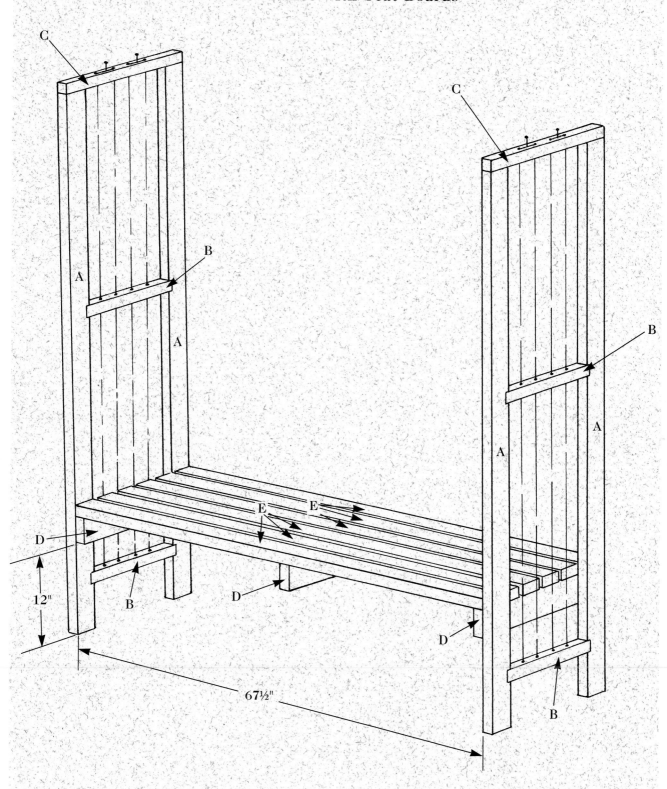

FIG. 71

Frame and Trim

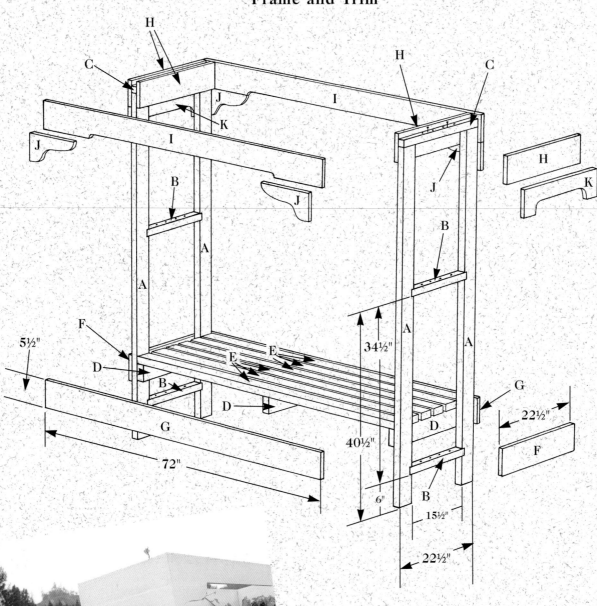

FIG. 72

Twining morning glories climb up the ends of the bench

BIRD FEEDER

The bird feeder is a finishing touch to the garden

This simple yet elegant bird feeder will attract a variety of birds throughout the seasons. Both children and adults will enjoy coaxing wildlife into their backyard. Using a bird identification book and a pair of binoculars, the experience can be fun and educational for everyone involved.

MATERIALS LIST

A – end walls	¾" × 11½" × 12½"	(2)	pine/fir 1×12
B – floor	¾" × 10" × 14½"	(1)	pine/fir 1×12
C – side rails	¾" × 1½" × 14½"	(4)	pine/fir 1×2
D – side walls	¾" × ¾" × 4½"	(4)	pine/fir 1×2
E – roof slats	¼" × 1½" × 18"	(14)	cedar lath
F – roof flashing	2" × 18"	(1)	copper sheet
G – wooden beads	1"	(2)	
H – wooden candle cups	1"	(2)	

3d galvanized finish nails

4d galvanized finish nails

6d galvanized finish nails

¾" × #18 brass escutcheon pins

wood filler

3" × #8 deck screws

exterior primer/sealer, paint, or stain

Filling the feeder to coax in feathered friends

ASSEMBLY INSTRUCTIONS

1. Begin construction of the bird feeder by cutting to size the pieces given in the materials list. Use the grid pattern to cut out the two end walls; see Fig. 73. Sand each piece smooth.

2. Attach the floor piece (**B**) to the bottom edge of each end wall (**A**) with four 4d galvanized finish nails on each side. To avoid splitting the wood, pre-drill the nail holes with a ¹⁄₁₆-inch drill bit. The bottom of the floor should be flush with the bottom of the end walls, leaving ¾ inch on each side of the end wall; see Fig. 74.

3. Next, attach the two lower side rails (**C**) to the edge of the floor with four 4d nails on each side. Also, secure the lower side rails to the end walls with two nails at each end. Nail through the front of the end walls into the side rails.

4. The small side walls (**D**) go on next and sit on top of the side rails (**C**) and against the back edge of the end walls (**A**). Use two 3d finish nails to attach each side wall to the end walls.

5. Attach the last two side rails. They sit on top of

End Wall Grid

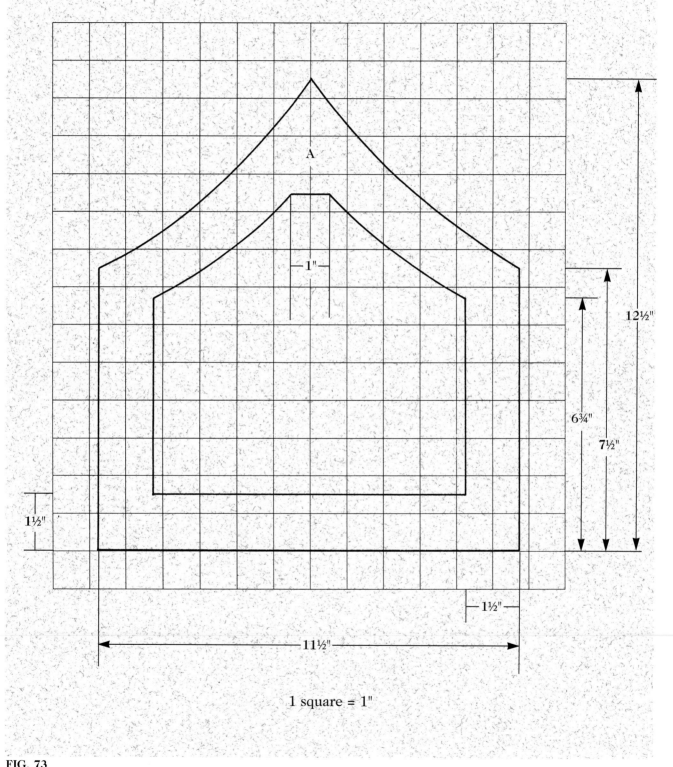

FIG. 73

Bird Feeder

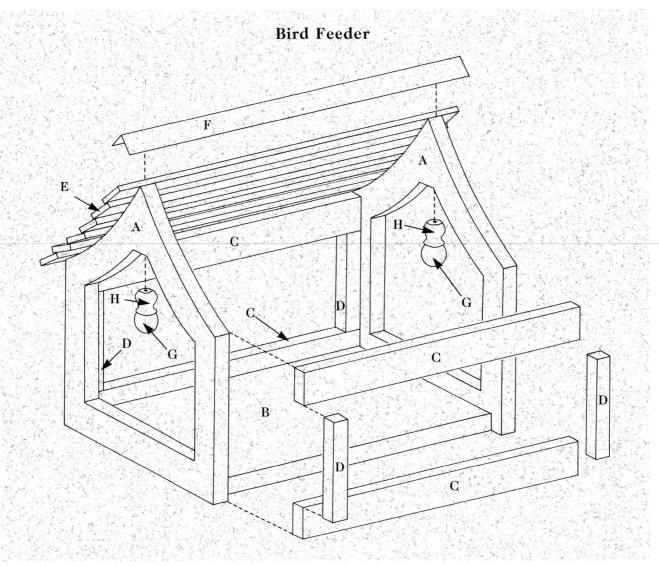

FIG. 74

the side walls and attach to the end walls with two 4d nails at each end. Nail through the end walls into the ends of the side rails.

6. Before attaching the roof, make sure all nails are countersunk and the holes filled with a wood filler. Apply any stain, paint or protective coating to the feeder now as it is easier than waiting until after the roof goes on. Apply any paint or protective coating you may want on the fourteen roof slats at this time as well.

7. Now attach the roof slats (**E**) to the feeder in a "shingle" fashion. The first slat is nailed on at the lower edge of the roof, overhanging the side by ½ inch and overhanging the two end walls by 1 inch. The slats are attached to the end wall peaks using two brass escutcheon pins per slat. Nail near the uphill edge of the slat so that the next "shingle" will cover the pins. Repeat this up the roof, overlapping each slat approximately ¼ inch (it might help to pre-position each slat on the roof before nailing, to get the spacing correct). You should end up at or near the roof's peak, using seven slats per side.

8. Finish the roof with a piece of copper flashing

(**F**). Cut a 2 × 18-inch strip of copper sheet using a utility knife (large sheets of copper are available at most craft stores). Create the right-angle bend in the strip by placing it halfway over the edge of a sturdy table (make sure the table's edge is not rounded). Use two pieces of 1×2 at least 18 inches or longer to bend the strip in half lengthwise. Hold down one half of the strip on the edge of the table with one of the 1×2s, while using the other one to evenly press down on the half of the strip hanging over the edge of the table.

9. Secure the copper flashing to the bird feeder roof using four brass escutcheon pins, two per side, nailed into the peak area of the two end walls.

The classic design of this feeder will add charm to your garden

10. As a final decorative touch, add a finial to each end of your bird feeder. Most craft stores carry wooden beads (**G**) and small turned wooden "candle cups" (**H**). Each generally comes pre-drilled with a hole, if not, use a ³⁄₃₂-inch drill bit to drill a hole through the center of each piece. Combine them as shown in Fig. 74. Slide a 6d galvanized finish nail up through the center of each piece, then lightly tap the nail into the center of the one-inch flat area in the end wall opening. Finish both finials to match the rest of the bird feeder.

11. Finally, drill a hole in the bottom center of the feeder and mount it on the end of a 3-inch round fence post using a 3-inch deck screw and an offset screwdriver.

Part Three

Gardening Basics

As with most projects, gardening will be an enjoyable and successful experience if you have the correct tools, techniques and knowledge to tackle the job. Mother Nature occasionally throws us an unexpected curve ball, but for the most part the following basic gardening techniques will help ensure a rewarding gardening experience. Written clearly and simply, these basics will show you how to grow a healthy, productive garden, and you can pass this knowledge on to your children as they participate in the planting, care and harvest of your family garden.

Compost in the making

Composting

Every year, our gardens and kitchens generate massive amounts of organic waste. Grass clippings, garden debris and kitchen peelings are just a few of our vegetative throw-outs. Quite often, these materials are either burned or put in the trash and sent to landfills. With increasing burn bans, due to air pollution and diminishing landfill space, it makes sense to recycle this organic refuse into soil-enriching compost. When added to the soil, this dark, rich humus holds moisture, provides good drainage and contributes beneficial nutrients to the plants.

Microorganisms are the workhorse of the compost pile. These beneficial bacteria will thrive in your compost if you provide them with the proper combination of organic waste, water and air circulation. As the microorganisms decompose the pile, the frenzy of bacterial activity generates heat, often between 120 and 150 degrees Fahrenheit, in the center of the pile. The heat kills many weed seeds and disease spores. To further speed the decaying process, chop your large garden debris and woody stems into small pieces. Adding high-nitrogen materials to the mix, in the form of manure, fishmeal or blood meal, is optional; however, it will speed the decomposition process and add nutrients to the soil.

Compost bins are not necessary, although they do contain the debris and make the garden look tidy (see page 69 for Compost Bin instructions). Start your compost by compiling a variety of organic materials in the bin. Layer the debris to ensure the ingredients are evenly distributed throughout the heap. Begin with several inches of coarse plant waste on the bottom, such as corn stalks or small twigs. This coarse material will provide air circulation at the bottom of the pile. The next layer will be an inch or two of manure followed by a sprinkling of topsoil. Repeat these layers again, starting with a 9- to 12-inch layer of vegetative waste containing approximately equal amounts of dry, brown materials such as leaves and straw, and green materials such as grass clippings and kitchen waste. Sprinkle water on the layers as you build up the pile. Once the pile is your desired height, make a concave depression at the top to aid in capturing rainwater. During dry spells, water the compost to keep it evenly moist but not waterlogged.

Use a spading fork or pitchfork to occasionally turn the pile. This will replenish the air supply in the heap and ensure the materials that were on the outside of the pile are turned in to the center.

A properly maintained compost pile will not have an offensive odor.

Within a few months, your compost will be a dark, rich, crumbly soil amendment that is ready to use. The following is a list of some organic waste materials that are suitable for making compost. As a precaution, always burn diseased or insect-infested materials.

Leaves: Scatter them in thin layers so they don't form a thick mat and decompose slowly. Better yet, chop them first with a chipper/shredder or lawnmower.

Lawn clippings: Scatter them in thin layers so they don't mat down.

Woody stems: Always shred large or woody garden debris, such as corn stalks, with a chipper/shredder.

Kitchen garbage: All vegetable kitchen waste is suitable, as well as coffee grounds and eggshells. Large pieces or woody pieces, such as corncobs, will decompose faster if they are ground up or cut into small chunks. Fats, grease, bones, meat and dairy products are all unsuitable for the compost bin.

Manure: Optional; however, it adds nitrogen to the mix and speeds decomposition.

Soil: Soil, sprinkled throughout the compost heap, will introduce beneficial bacteria and worms to the mix.

Weeds: Avoid putting perennial or noxious weeds in your compost. Keep to young, annual weeds that have not gone to seed. Although the heat of the compost will kill many seeds, it may not destroy them all.

Hay and straw: Fluff out the bale sections and mix thoroughly with other compost ingredients so it doesn't form a thick mat. Chopped hay and straw will decompose faster.

Soil Preparation

A lush, productive garden is the result of well-prepared garden soil. Whether your soil is too porous with sand or too heavy with clay, it can be improved to promote vigorous plant growth.

The key to wonderful soil, and therefore wonderful crops, is the addition of organic material in the form of peat, compost, well-rotted manure and cover crops. Organic matter (or humus) helps sandy soils by improving its water-retention abilities, which in turn keeps nutrients from leaching through the soil. Clay soils are lightened by organic matter allowing air and water to penetrate to the roots. Even loamy soils, which are a combination of sand, silt and clay, will be further improved by the addition of nutrient-rich organic matter.

If you are developing a new garden, start in early spring by staking out the garden's perimeter. Remove the sod and any stones, rubble and roots from the area. Determine whether the soil is dry enough to work by squeezing a handful of it into a ball. Break the ball apart with your fingers;

Preparing the soil for late summer planting

if it remains sticky and muddy, the soil is too wet; if it breaks apart easily, the soil is ready to work.

Once the soil can be worked, start your garden preparations by adding the amendments. Scatter equal amounts of compost, peat and well-rotted manure over the surface of the soil until it is covered with a layer 2 to 4 inches deep (if necessary, an application of lime can also be added at this time). If your garden is large, use a tiller to incorporate the amendments into the soil. However, small and medium-size gardens can be deeply cultivated by hand using a spade or a spading fork. Loosening and incorporating the amendments deep into the soil will encourage vigorous root growth. Rake the area smooth and quickly define the paths so the actual growing areas are not accidentally walked on and compressed. Your garden is now ready for planting.

Planting a cover crop in the fall will prevent erosion during the winter months and further increase the organic matter in the soil when it is turned under in the spring. Rye grass is an excellent cover crop, as well as oats, buckwheat and clover.

Various seed-starting supplies

Starting Seeds

Every spring it's amazing to watch tiny, hard seeds turn into magnificent, huge plants in a matter of months. This remarkable transformation will only occur, however, if you supply the seeds with a proper growing environment. Whether you start your seeds indoors or out, you can increase their germination and survival rate by following a few simple steps.

Starting Seeds Indoors

In areas where the growing season is short, give your long-season crops a head start by planting the seeds indoors in trays or flats. A variety of areas in your house are suitable for starting seeds. A bright window, for instance, can accommodate

two or three flats. Even a dark basement or insulated garage can offer a growing area if you illuminate the flats with grow lights or fluorescent lights (for best results, position the lights 6 to 8 inches above the foliage). Another consideration is warmth. Seeds generally need a warm environment for good germination (between 68 and 86 degrees Fahrenheit). If you plan to start your seeds in a basement or garage, consider using electric heating cables to provide bottom heat. Heating cables and mats made specifically for starting seeds are available through catalogs and garden centers.

Always keep your planting materials and tools extremely clean. Young seedlings are particularly susceptible to damping off. This condition is caused by various soil and waterborne fungi which attack the seedlings, withering their roots and stems in the process. These fungi can decimate an entire flat of seedlings very quickly. Reduce the chances of an infestation by using sterile potting soil and sterilizing your pots and trays in a 10 percent solution of bleach and then rinsing them with clean water. Other preventive measures include keeping your growing area well ventilated, sowing your seeds thinly and avoiding the tendency to overwater.

Begin by filling your flats or trays to the rim with potting soil and lightly rapping them against a hard surface to settle the soil. Make sure the label on your potting soil bag specifically designates the mix for starting seeds. Use a fine spray to thoroughly moisten the growing medium. Sow large seeds one by one into the individual cells of the tray. Fine seeds will need to be lightly scattered over the surface of the soil. Refer to the instructions on the back of the individual seed packets for planting depths. Gently sprinkle the appropriate amount of potting soil over the seeds that require darkness for germination. Some seeds need light to germinate and will not require a covering of soil. Label each flat as you finish sowing the seeds. Keep your seed trays evenly moist (but not soggy) at all times. Check on the flats twice a day, especially if you are using heating cables, so they never dry out.

When the small seeds have germinated and are large enough to handle by their leaves, prick out (transplant) the individual seedlings to new flats or small pots. Water the newly transplanted starts with a fine spray and place them in a bright area to continue growing for several more days.

Once their roots have become established and the shock of being transplanted is over, gradually harden off the seedlings. This is a process of acclimating them to cooler conditions; first to a cold frame or temporary cloche, and then to their final outdoor location. The transition from your house to a cold frame should be made over the course of several days. Place the flats in a cold frame for a few hours on the first day, then gradually work up to leaving them in overnight. It's a good idea to set out several mouse traps. On cold nights, mice are quickly attracted to the warmth and shelter of a cold frame complete with young tasty sprouts!

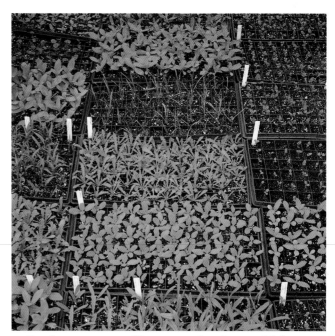

Tender young seedlings growing in a cold frame

If weather conditions are below freezing at night, the flats should always be brought indoors. If temperatures are above freezing but still cold, flats can be left out if heating cables or lights are used to elevate the temperature inside the frame (chicken brooder lamps work well). For added protection, lay blankets over the frame for insulation if nighttime temperatures will be around freezing. (As a precaution, bring tender annuals, such as tomatoes, indoors on these cold nights.)

You may have to deal with the opposite problem during the day. Even on cool days, if the sun is shining the temperature inside a closed cold frame can soar. Make sure the frame is left open a crack on bright days for proper ventilation.

As planting time draws near, continue to harden off the seedlings by leaving the cold frame open at night.

The Family Garden sundial and sailboat projects require large amounts of alyssum and lobelia. Buying large numbers of bedding plants from nurseries can be costly; however, starting them yourself from seed is relatively inexpensive and easy.

To create your own alyssum and lobelia starts, you will need several plastic plug flat trays available at most garden centers (we use trays that have 72 1-inch cells per flat). Fill the flats to their rims with sterile potting soil appropriate for starting seeds. Evenly moisten the soil with a fine spray of water. Then, very lightly, sprinkle the seeds across the surface of the soil so that 3 to 5 seeds cover each square inch. Both alyssum and lobelia need light to germinate, so don't cover the seed with additional soil. Put the flats in a warm area with plenty of light and good air circulation. Providing the flats with bottom heat from heating cables will speed germination. Always keep the soil evenly moist.

If you scatter the seeds thinly, no pricking out is necessary. The seedlings can grow on in the flats until they are ready to be planted outdoors in the garden. However, if some cells are overcrowded, which may happen with the tiny lobelia seeds, simply prick out small groups of seedlings and transplant them to a new plug flat filled with soil. Lobelia and alyssum are quite susceptible to damping off and may require a light application of fungicide.

Use the information on the back of the seed packets to plan your planting times. Lobelia takes longer to germinate and grows more slowly than alyssum. If you want them to bloom at approximately the same time, their starting dates will need to be about six weeks apart. Once the seeds have germinated and are well established, the young plants can be hardened off and moved into a cold frame to continue growing until it's time to plant them out in the garden.

Planting Out

Once all danger of frost has passed and your garden soil is prepared, you can plant out your seedlings. Choose a mild day with overcast skies so the young plants can adapt to their new surroundings without the additional stress of the hot sun. Thoroughly water the seedlings before you remove them from their containers. Use a small hand trowel to dig a hole for each seedling, spacing them according to the

Planting out a late crop of lettuce

guidelines given on the seed packet. Plant the seedlings to the same depth that they were in their containers. Firm the soil around the base of each plant and water them in to settle the soil around the root balls.

Starting Seeds Outdoors

After all danger of frost has passed and the garden site is prepared, you can plant your seeds. Rake the soil smooth to prepare the seed bed. If you intend to plant in rows, use a length of string stretched between two stakes to keep your lines straight. With the point of a hoe or shovel, make a shallow furrow along the length of string. Plant large seeds by dropping them one by one along the furrow at their correct spacing. Scatter small seeds as evenly as possible along the line. Cover the seeds to the depth recommended on the seed packet. Gently firm the soil in place so it has good contact with the seeds. Water the soil and never let the germinating seeds dry out. Remove the strings and place row markers at the ends of the lines to indicate the placement of the different plant varieties (see Row Markers on page 94).

The moist, nutrient-rich soil you provide for your flower and vegetable seeds will also be enjoyed by weed seeds. As they germinate simultaneously, keep the tenacious weed seedlings in check so they don't overrun the garden.

Thinning

Large seeds, such as beans, peas, corn and pumpkins, are easy to sow in the garden. However, small seeds, such as carrots, lettuce and endive, are difficult to sow individually and often come up in close groupings. To prevent overcrowding as the plants grow, some seedlings will need to be removed or "thinned."

Thinning is best done when the seedlings are still small and their roots have not become intertwined. Choose a day when the weather is mild, so the heat of the sun does not stress the plants.

Sowing carrot seeds in a freshly prepared bed

Moisten the soil before you begin. Look the bed of seedlings over for the strongest and healthiest, as you determine which plants will stay. Hold the soil firmly in place near the base of the seedlings that will remain and gently pull out the other seedlings in the area. Without the brace of the surrounding plants, those that are left may need the soil drawn up around their stems for support. If their roots have become too entwined to pull them out safely, use scissors to snip off the unwanted seedlings at the soil line.

A lesson on thinning radishes

Thin out the row until the plants are properly spaced for their variety. This information can be found on individual seed packets. Finish by lightly watering the plants to settle the soil back around their roots.

Many seedlings that were removed with their roots intact can be transplanted to other areas of the garden or used to fill in bare spots along the row. Carrots can be thinned in a two-step process. Do an initial thinning so the plants are spaced about ½ to 1 inch apart. Then, halfway through the growing season, harvest every other one and enjoy the delicacy of sweet, young baby carrots. The remaining carrots will now be properly spaced to grow on to maturity without being overcrowded. Spinach is also delicious at this young tender stage. By composting the leftover thinnings, not a single plant will go to waste, and the remaining plants will grow on and reach their full potential.

Getting the job of watering done twice as fast

Watering

Water is necessary for all plants to survive. Taken up by the roots of the plant, water carries with it essential nutrients which maintain good plant growth. Weather and soil conditions are the determining factors in how much water your garden will require. Every gardener must carefully observe their own garden and decide when and how much to water.

Sandy soils, which have a porous structure, will require frequent watering. Unfortunately this may leach away important nutrients. Combat these problems by adding organic matter to the soil. In heavy clay soils, water percolates slowly. If it is applied too quickly, it will run off the soil surface rather than soaking into the root zone. Use soaker hoses or a sprinkler that delivers a lighter volume of water, and add organic matter to lighten the soil.

Germinating seeds and young seedlings can be easily washed away with heavy watering, so, as a general rule, apply small amounts of water frequently. Larger, established plants should be watered less frequently but receive a thorough soaking. This will encourage roots to grow deeper into the soil instead of growing close to the surface where there is a greater risk of them drying out. No matter what your weather conditions are or the condition of your soil structure, all gardens will benefit from a layer of moisture-retaining mulch.

The best time to water your garden is in the morning. If you wait until the afternoon, much of the water is wasted to evaporation. If you water in the evening, the foliage may remain wet throughout the night, which increases the possibility of fungal infestations brought on by prolonged damp conditions.

Mulching

A simple layer of mulch can save you time and energy and it promotes healthy plant growth. Mulching materials can be organic, such as grass

barrier between the fruit and the damaging soil.

Apply organic mulches in a layer two to four inches thick. Because of its insulating effects, let the soil warm in the spring before you mulch, and apply it while the soil is still moist (but not wet). To prevent damping off, keep the mulch pulled back from the stems of very young seedlings until they become established. At season's end, organic mulches can be turned under, adding moisture-retaining humus to the soil structure.

The following is a short list of mulching materials and comments on their characteristics.

Organic Mulch

Grass clippings: Grass clippings make a terrific mulch because they're free and readily available. Use a thin, two-inch layer of clippings. A thick layer may ferment and reduce air circulation to the soil below. Only use clippings from lawns free of weed killer.

Straw: Straw is clean and easy to broadcast and contains relatively few weed seeds. However, grain kernels left behind by the harvester may germinate but are easily plucked from the loose mulch.

Wood chips, chopped bark, sawdust: Wood products break down slowly and temporarily rob nitrogen from the soil. Use wood products mainly on paths.

Chopped leaves: Chopped leaves create a light and fluffy earth-toned mulch (whole leaves tend to form a mat which can reduce air circulation to the soil). There are no weed seeds to contend with and they enrich the soil when they are turned under at season's end.

Peat moss: Peat moss is wonderful for adding humus to the soil; however, it can be an expen-

clippings, or inorganic, such as a layer of black plastic film or landscape fabric. Discovering the benefits and drawbacks of each material will help you choose the best mulch for your garden.

Weeds are a constant problem in most gardens. Mulching your garden beds and dirt paths will substantially reduce your amount of weeding. Both organic and inorganic mulches suppress weed seeds from germinating. Those that do germinate in organic mulches are easily pulled from the fluffy layer.

As the summer wears on, the baking sun and blowing wind quickly evaporate soil moisture. Mulches insulate the soil from these damaging elements, keeping soil temperatures cool and preventing moisture evaporation. Throughout the growing season, mulches also keep the garden looking groomed and orderly. A dirt path covered with a good layer of mulch, for instance, will stay relatively weed free. Additionally, overhead watering will not create a muddy walkway.

Vegetables growing close to the ground are often splashed with mud and sometimes rest on the damp earth which can encourage rot. Mulches prevent the splashing and provide a dry

sive mulch, depending on the size of your garden. Peat should be pulled away from plant stems because its moisture-retaining qualities may cause fungus and rot. It also adds to the acidity of the soil, so a neutralizing application of lime may be needed once it has been turned under (use a soil-testing kit to determine your soil's pH value; it should be about pH 6.5).

Hulls: Various hulls can be used as mulch and they add interesting textures to the garden. Depending on their size, some hulls may be slow to decompose. Hazelnut shells, for instance, make an attractive, semi-permanent mulch for paths.

Compost: Compost is one of the best mulching materials because it's free, and it adds nutrients and humus to the soil. Like peat moss, it should be kept away from plant stems because its moisture-retaining qualities may cause fungus and rot.

Crushed rock: Crushed rock is wonderful for mulching permanent paths. Use it in combination with landscape fabric for a path that drains easily and stays relatively weed free.

Inorganic Mulch

Black plastic: Using black plastic as a mulch keeps weeds under control and warms the soil for early-season crops. Heat-loving plants, such as peppers, flourish in the warmed soil. The surface is non-porous so it is beneficial to place soaker hoses under the plastic. Anchor the sides of the plastic by burying the edges with soil. Cut slits to plant through with a serrated knife. If you decided not to put in drip irrigation, water through the slits.

Landscape fabric: Landscape fabric is a ground covering made from woven strands of plastic that allows water to penetrate, but suppresses weeds. It is very useful as a permanent mulch, especially when used in combination with a top dressing. For example, a top dressing of gravel is great for paths.

Pronged hand cultivator

Cultivating

In beds that aren't mulched, cultivating will break up the soil surface, which keeps down weeds and aerates the soil. In turn, your plants will grow unhindered and water will easily percolate down to the roots rather than running off the encrusted soil surface.

While young seedlings are becoming established, so too are young weeds. As they grow, they compete with one another for water, nutrients and garden space. If left unchecked, weeds will grow faster, leaving your garden plants shaded out and weak. Your best defense is to cultivate regularly while weeds are small and easily uprooted.

There are many varieties of cultivating tools available through catalogs and garden centers. They all have their special attributes, but the two most common are the hoe and the pronged hand cultivator. The hoe is perfect for loosening soil in between crop rows, while the hand cultivator works well around individual plants. Use both to lightly break up the soil surface to a depth of a ½ to 1 inch. It's best to hand weed as you work in closer to the base of individual plants; you may run the risk of clipping off young seedlings or disturbing established roots with cultivating tools. Fleshy root crops growing just below the soil surface are especially vulnerable to the nick of a metal tine. Children should hand weed until they are old enough to easily handle cultivating tools. It would be heartbreaking to have a prized plant they nurtured all summer long accidentally damaged by an unforgiving tine.

Floating Row Covers

Organic plant protection is particularly important in a family garden so children are not exposed to pesticides. Protecting crops from insect damage, without the use of pesticides, is simple with floating row covers. This fine mesh fabric is so lightweight, it can be draped over the plants without hindering their growth. With the exception of plants that need pollination from insects, row covers can remain on most low-growing crops until maturity.

Cabbages, cauliflower, radishes and carrots are just a few plants that greatly benefit from floating row covers. The fabric will help prevent

damage from cabbage root maggots, carrot rust flies and a host of other insects.

Anchor the edges of the loosely draped fabric with stones or small piles of soil. If you prefer, it can be stretched over hoops, creating a protective tunnel. Except for weeding and harvesting, there is no need to remove the cover because water and light easily pass through the fabric.

Row covers provide extra benefits for the early spring garden. In many cases, it will help protect the plants from unexpected light frosts. It also slightly elevates the air and soil temperature, giving the young plants a head start in the spring.

Harvesting

The small seeds planted weeks, or even months, earlier, have grown into lush plants and are now laden with produce! Harvesting begins in the spring with early crops of spinach, lettuce and herbs, and carries right on through the growing season. Depending on your climate and ingenuity, it's possible to have something to harvest from your garden year-round. However, peak harvest time is late summer through early autumn.

Have a well-thought-out plan for your produce. Even a small garden can produce an overwhelming abundance of vegetables. Eating fresh veggies straight from the garden is a special treat at this time of year, but consider freezing, canning or storing root crops in a cellar for healthy meals during the long winter months. If you have extra produce, share the bounty with a "gardenless" neighbor. Children love to load up their wagons and deliver homegrown gifts, especially pumpkins, to their friends.

Floating row cover protecting the vegetables

The joy of harvesting

Part Four

Harvest Projects
for
Children

By mid to late summer, the tiny seeds your children helped sow in early spring have matured into large plants bearing hundreds of flowers and vegetables. Their long and patient wait has finally paid off; it's harvest time! A time of excitement, when they find a wonderfully shaped gourd or huge pumpkin previously hidden from view by the dense foliage; a time of learning and creativity, when they try new recipes and craft projects with their produce; and a time of discovery, when they sample the unfamiliar tastes of edible flowers and new vegetables. The following projects will show your children ways to enjoy gardening far beyond the boundaries of the garden beds.

PUMPKINS

Growing pumpkins is a project that starts in the spring and isn't finished until Halloween. In the process, your children will learn about seeds, plants and patience; and in the end have fun crafting a jack-o'-lantern.

Pumpkins are simple to grow. They germinate readily and the large seeds are easy for small fingers to handle. Choose a sunny location with fertile soil where the sprawling vines can grow outwards 6–8 feet. Plant the seeds in late spring after all danger of frost has passed. For specific growing instructions, refer to the individual seed packets. Provide the plants with plenty of water during the growing season. Once the small pumpkins begin to appear on the vines, place a board under the fruit to prevent rot. When the pumpkins are bright orange, use pruning shears to cut them from the vine, leaving a three-inch stem. Now the creative projects can begin.

Pumpkin Carving

Pumpkin carving is a fall tradition that the entire family can participate in and enjoy. There are a variety of methods for carving pumpkins as well as an endless number of carving designs. Most pumpkin-carving tools are sharp, so parental assistance is necessary to help young carvers enjoy the project without getting hurt. Very young children can participate by drawing designs on their pumpkins with felt-tip pens, or pressing cookie-cutter shapes into the skin. An adult can then carve

A carrot-nosed jack-o'-lantern illuminating the fall garden

the cutting tool needs to be to maneuver the intricate cut lines.

The third lantern pumpkin pictured (on the right) was also carved in the traditional manner. However, the eyebrows and nose were created with wood-carving tools. Small gouges made in the orange skin revealed the cream-colored flesh below. When illuminated with a candle, these translucent areas glowed while the light from the eyes and mouth shined brightly.

Pumpkin Scratching

Pumpkin scratching is a relatively safe project for young children. With the point of a nail, they can scratch their names or pictures onto young pumpkins that are still on the vine. As the pumpkins grow, the scratches callous-over, creating tan-colored lines. Unlike carved pumpkins, that begin to wilt and rot within a few days, scratched pumpkins can decorate your porch for weeks.

Pumpkin scratching works best on very young pumpkins. The immature fruit should be approximately 6–8 inches long with light green skin that feels waxy to the touch. If you wait until the pumpkin is dark green and the skin becomes hard and shiny, the scaring will not be as pronounced.

With the point of a sterilized nail, draw only on the side that is facing up. Turning or moving the pumpkin while it is still attached to the vine may cause the stem to break. Scratch through the surface of the skin, being careful not to puncture the fruit itself. Use small cross-hatch lines to fill in sections, rather than scratching away large areas of skin which may leave the pumpkin susceptible to rot.

Very young children can participate by gently

out the design for them. Everyone, however, can join in the gooey fun of pulling out the pulp and seeds!

Carving tools can range from a simple kitchen knife to a set of small saws specifically designed for pumpkin carving (available at craft stores). You can experiment with different techniques using cookie cutters, drill bits, wood carving tools, and mat knives.

Three different techniques were used in making the pumpkins pictured above. The lantern to the left was created with a ⅜-inch drill bit and a biscuit cutter (small cookie cutters can also be used). A young child can score the pumpkin skin with the biscuit cutter, positioning the cutter where they want the lantern windows. An adult can then cut out the window holes with a knife. For extra detail, use a drill to make a series of holes around the windows.

Older children can carve pumpkins in the traditional manner by drawing a face on the pumpkin with a felt-tip marker and cutting out the design with a pumpkin-carving tool (as was done to create the middle pumpkin pictured). Just remember, the smaller your design, the smaller

pressing small cookie cutters into the pumpkin's skin. Older children might enjoy pre-planning a design that incorporates both pumpkin scratching and carving. For example, they may create a face by scratching in eyebrows and hair while the pumpkin is young and green. Once the pumpkin turns orange and has been harvested, they can carve in the eyes, nose and mouth.

A scratched pumpkin face from start to finish: on the vine, a few weeks later and in an autumn display

GOURDS

Growing, Harvesting and Curing

Every gourd is unique. Their varying shapes and sizes make them fun to grow and perfect for crafting projects. The best gourds for crafting are the large dipper, bottle or bushel gourds (*Lagenaria siceraria*). Their vigorous vines can take over a small garden, so carefully plan their placement (see Arbor on page 13).

Gourds need a long warm growing season. In cool climates the seeds will need to be started indoors. After all danger of frost has past, transplant the seedlings to the garden being careful not to disturb the tender roots. If your growing season is long; seeds may be planted directly into the garden once the soil has warmed. Gourd seeds may rot rather than germinate if planted in cold, wet soil.

Harvest the gourds when they are fully mature. This can be determined by watching the tendril that grows nearest to the stem of the gourd. When the tendril turns brown the gourd is ready for picking. Cut the gourd off the vine, leaving one or two inches of stem. Harvest gourds carefully because any bruising or punctures to the skin are potential areas for rot.

Bring your gourds indoors to cure. Wash them

with a household disinfectant to remove dirt and to kill any bacteria or fungi that may encourage rot. Choose an area with good air circulation. To ensure even drying, arrange them so they are not touching one another and turn them often. Gourds will change color and mold may appear as they dry, but as long as the shell remains hard this will not harm the gourd. If soft spots develop, discard the rotting gourd so it will not infect the others. Small gourds can dry in several weeks, while large ones may take several months. When they are light and fully dry, you can begin preparing them for project use.

Before you cut or paint your gourds, their outer skin must be softened and removed. Soak them in warm water for one hour and then wrap them in wet towels overnight. Once the skin is soft, scrape it off with a knife and sand them smooth with fine sandpaper.

Birdhouse

Attracting birds into your backyard is fun, educational and beneficial to the garden. Your whole family will enjoy watching birds choose their nesting sites and raising their broods. During the summer months, many birds, such as swallows, will consume thousands of garden-devouring insects and mosquitoes.

A variety of birds can be easily attracted to your landscape by providing them with a source of water, food and shelter. Building a gourd birdhouse is an easy first step in coaxing these feathered friends into residency. Start by going to your local library and researching the common birds of your area, and decide which ones you want to entice into your backyard. Make sure your gourds are the correct dimensions for the birds' housing requirements. Use the chart below as a basic guide.

Housing Requirements

Species	Floor size	Height	Entrance above floor	Diameter of entrance	Height above ground
Chickadee	4" × 4"	8" – 10"	6" – 8"	1⅛"	6' – 15'
Downy woodpecker	4" × 4"	9" – 12"	6" – 8"	1¼"	6' – 20'
House wren	4" × 4"	6" – 8"	1" – 6"	1" – 1¼"	6' – 10'
Titmouse	4" × 4"	8" – 10"	6" – 8"	1¼"	6' – 15'
Tree swallow	5" × 5"	6"	1" – 5"	1½"	10' – 15'
Violet-green swallow	5" × 5"	6"	1" – 5"	1½"	10' – 15'

Children decorated these birdhouses with acrylic craft paints. The green basecoats match the leaves while the colorful designs make them unique.

Birds often return year after year to their chosen nesting sites and may reuse a birdhouse if the old nesting material is cleaned out. Use the hooked end of a coat hanger to pull out the nesting material through the entrance hole. If you prefer, grow a new birdhouse every year.

MATERIALS LIST

large well-cured gourd (*Lagenaria siceraria*)

strong twine or leather thong

assorted acrylic craft paints

exterior polyurethane

ASSEMBLY INSTRUCTIONS

1. At the specified height, drill the appropriate size entrance hole in the side of the gourd.
2. With the end of a coat hanger, pull the dried pulp and seeds out through the entrance hole.
3. Use a drill bit no larger than ¼ inch to drill across the top of the gourd an inch or two below the stem. Thread the twine or thong hanger through the holes and tie the ends off with a square knot.
4. With the same bit, drill four or five drainage holes in the bottom of the gourd.

5. Your children can now paint and decorate the outer surface of the gourd. Once the decorations are finished, seal the surface with two coats of exterior polyurethane. Complete this project during the winter months so the polyurethane has plenty of time to cure.

Gourd Craft Projects

Throughout history, different cultures have used gourds to craft an amazing array of items, ranging from ceremonial masks, musical instruments and toys to an endless variety of containers. Gourds are a popular crafting material because their hard, woody shells can be cut, drilled, sanded and painted. The following are just a few craft ideas your family can work on together. Each gourd, with its unique shape, will bring to mind a different project.

Maracas

Rattles and maracas are easy to make and children enjoy decorating and shaking them. Two similarly shaped gourds were used to make the

one, through the holes and into the gourds. Fill the gourds with a good amount of seed so it has a loud rattle. Apply a small amount of wood glue to a ¼-inch doweling pin and insert the pin into the hole so it is flush with the gourd's surface. Once the glue is dry, your children can decorate their projects. Protect the decorations by applying two coats of exterior polyurethane to the entire surface. (Note: Painted or sealed gourds are not appropriate for use as baby rattles or young toddler toys.)

Containers

The large bulbous base of most gourds is perfect for crafting containers. Simply cut the neck from a dry gourd using a hacksaw or coping saw. Remove the dried pulp and seeds from the interior. After sanding the cut edges smooth, the container is ready for your children to paint. Save the neck and use it as a lid, or add extra details such as a small wire handle. Once the containers are complete, use them to hold potpourri, dried flower arrangements, marble collections or small toys.

An assortment of projects made from gourds (from left to right): maracas, a birdhouse, a container with a wire handle, a gourd beginning to change color as it dries, and a small gourd container complete with its own lid

maracas pictured. Drill a ¼-inch hole in the end of each dry gourd just to the side of the stem. Set out bowls of popcorn seeds or small dried beans and have your children drop the seeds, one by

EDIBLE FLOWERS

Brighten everyday meals with colorful, edible flowers. Their delicate petals add visual interest and a variety of flavors to salads, main dishes and desserts. Children are fascinated by the idea of eating flowers and they enjoy creating colorful garnishes for the family dinner table.

The following projects use four edible flower varieties that are all easy-to-grow annuals: viola (either *Viola odorata*, *Viola tricolor* or *Viola cornuta*), calendula (*Calendula officinalis*), sunflower (*Helianthus annuus*) and nasturtium (*Tropaeolum majus*). For specific growing instructions, refer to the back of the individual seed packets.

Each flower has its own flavor. The petals of violas, sunflowers and calendulas are mild, while

Viola (Viola tricolor)

Calendula (Calendula officinalis)

Nasturtium (Tropaeolum majus)

Sunflower (Helianthus annuus)

nasturtiums have a distinctive peppery taste. They offer a brilliant range of colors from light yellow and orange to deep red and purple. Let your children create colorful meals with these confetti-like petals.

A Note of Warning: As a precaution, consume edible flowers in small quantities. Children should be taught to pick and eat edible flowers only while an adult is supervising. As with all foods, some people can have allergic reactions, and edible flowers are no exception. Assist your children as they try new edibles in the garden. *Not all flowers are edible!* Correctly identify each edible flower and then gently rub a few petals on the wrists to check for an allergic reaction. If such a wrist test shows a sensitivity to a particular flower, the person or child should not eat it.

Garnishing Cupcakes

Decorating desserts with edible flowers is easy and the results are instantly rewarding for young children. Begin by making a batch of cupcakes and frosting them with a light-colored frosting (the flowers will show up better on light frosting). Then help them gather edible flowers from the garden. Choose flowers that are in good condition and in full bloom. Once you've returned to the kitchen, carefully check the flowers for any unwanted insects or bug damage. Place all the good flower heads on a table along with the cupcakes and watch the fun begin. Children can make confetti out of the flowers by gently pulling the petals off the heads. Large nasturtium and sunflower petals can be carefully ripped into small pieces or cut into long strips. When the flower petals and bits are ready, these garnishes can be sprinkled onto the cupcakes like confetti. Complete the decorations with the placement of a single viola flower in the center of each treat.

As a special touch to the dinner table, use the decorated cupcakes as a centerpiece. Children can gather extra flowers from the garden and place

Cupcakes decorated with edible flower "confetti"

them around the dessert platter. This colorful, edible arrangement is a fun project for children and will be enjoyed by the entire family.

Garnishing Salads

Children can help prepare dinner and have fun by garnishing salads with edible flowers. Plain green salads come alive with the addition of colorful, edible flower petals. By adding grated carrots, red cabbage slices and bright red tomato wedges, these salad creations will contain almost every color in a crayon box! Collect and prepare the flowers in the same manner as for garnishing cupcakes.

Violet Ice Cubes

Violet ice cubes, floating in light pink lemonade, just might be the perfect addition to a summertime birthday party. Edible flower ice cubes are so easy to make, children can do this project with very little adult supervision.

The night before you want to use the cubes, fill an ice cube tray half full of water and put it in the freezer to ice up. The next morning, your children can go out to the garden and collect enough violets for each cube to contain two flowers. Lightly

Violet ice cubes chilling drinks on a hot summer day

rinse the flowers and check for any unwanted bugs.

Remove the ice cube tray from the freezer and put the half-size cubes in a bowl and return them to the freezer. Your children can then place two flowers in the bottom of each cube divider in the tray. Once the tray is full of flowers, replace the half-size cubes to their positions in the tray and fill the remaining space with water (the half-size cubes keep the flowers from floating to the surface and ensure the blossoms will be in the center of each cube). Return the tray to the freezer until the cubes are frozen solid. These fancy ice cubes can be made with any edible flowers.

GARDEN PRODUCE

By midsummer, your garden will be overflowing with vegetables. It's a wonderful time of year when fresh garden snacks are always at hand. Even finicky eaters may find they prefer home-grown fresh baby carrots and sweet cherry tomatoes over store bought. The following projects and recipes introduce children to a variety of veg-etables and in the process encourage healthy eating habits.

Veggie Platter Face

This is one time it's O.K. for your kids to play with their food! Using chopped and sliced vegetables, children can create an edible veggie platter in the shape of a funny face, an animal or a colorful design.

Start by collecting a variety of vegetables from the garden. Wash them thoroughly and cut them into various shapes. All the cutting should be done by an adult; however, children can participate by breaking up some by hand—for example, breaking off small florets of broccoli or individual kernels of corn, or pulling curly parsley leaves off their stems.

Separate the colorful pieces into bowls and set them in the center of the table. After your children have washed their hands, give each one a plate and let the creativity begin!

The veggie face pictured has a sliced red cabbage head, rosy tomato cheeks, bean lips, corn kernel teeth, parsley hair, carrots for ears and a nose, summer squash eyebrows, cucumber and cherry tomato eyes, and sliced onion eyelashes. The possibilities are endless, and your children will laugh and munch their way through this fun project. Once their picture platters are complete, set out a bowl of vegetable dip and let them eat their masterpieces for snack time.

A funny face to feast on!

Garden Scrambled Eggs

6 eggs

⅓ cup milk

salt and pepper to taste

1 tablespoon butter or margarine

⅓ cup grated cheese

½ cup chopped vegetables (your choice: broccoli, green onion, spinach, green pepper, tomatoes, zucchini, chives, parsley)

Scrambled eggs provide a perfect first-time cooking experience for children because they are fast and easy to make. Create a nutritious meal by adding fresh vegetables and grated cheese.

Working in the kitchen around a hot stove will require adult supervision at all times. Children may also need the help of a step stool to comfortably reach the counter and stovetop. Start by collecting a variety of vegetables from the garden. Dice them into small pieces so they will cook quickly (or pre-steam). Children can participate by tearing apart some vegetables by hand, such as spinach and broccoli florets.

Once the vegetables are chopped and set aside, crack the eggs into a large mixing bowl. Children enjoy breaking the yokes with a fork and stirring the eggs until they are creamy yellow. Have them carefully measure and add the milk along with a dash of salt and pepper.

Heat a pan on the stove and melt the butter or margarine. Pour the eggs into the pan and let your children slowly stir the mixture. They can add the chopped vegetables and grated cheese as the eggs cook.

Harvest Stew

1 pound beef stew meat (cubed)

1 can tomato sauce (8 oz)

¼ cup flour

1 teaspoon salt

¼ teaspoon pepper

3 tablespoons oil

3 cups water

3 beef boullion cubes

2 bay leaves

1 onion (chopped)

2 celery stalks (chopped)

4 cups chopped garden vegetables (Choose any combination of the following vegetables that are ready to harvest from your garden: tomatoes, carrots, potatoes, peas, beans, rutabagas, parsley, zucchini, turnips, corn.)

This recipe is "kid-tested," and they always ask for more! In early September, your garden will likely have most of the vegetable ingredients for this recipe. Harvest Stew is perfect for combining the abilities of children of all ages. Start by having them collect the appropriate vegetables from the garden. Young children can easily snap beans while older children can use a potato peeler to prepare the root crops. They can all help to measure and stir the ingredients into the stew pot.

In a plastic bag, shake the beef cubes together with the ¼ cup flour, salt and pepper. Heat the oil in a large stew pot and brown the beef (working around hot oil is dangerous and should only be done by an adult). Stir in the water, tomato sauce, boullion cubes, onion, celery and bay leaves. Cover and simmer until the meat is tender, about 1 hour. Add the chopped vegetables and simmer until they are tender, approximately 30 minutes. For thick stew, combine 2 tablespoons flour with ¼ cup water in a jar with a lid and shake well. Stir in and simmer until the stew thickens.

DRIED FLOWERS

Growing dried flowers is easy and the harvest will supply your family with an abundance of material to make floral craft projects. Young gardeners can participate throughout the process of growing, harvesting, drying and crafting, making the experience both fun and educational.

Dried flowers thrive in full sun and average garden soil. Annuals (plants that complete their entire life cycle in one season) are the easiest to grow and tend to be prolific bloomers. The seeds can be started indoors and transplanted to the garden after all danger of frost has passed, or they can be sown directly into the garden once the soil has warmed. For best results, refer to the specific instructions on the individual seed packets.

As harvest time draws near and flowers are in full bloom, protect delicate petals from water damage by hand-watering plants at their base.

Harvest flowers in midmorning, after the dew has dried. Cut each flower so a good length of stem remains (you can always cut them shorter for specific projects). Once cut, spread them out on a work area and sort them into their separate colors and varieties. Children are very good at sorting flowers by color and shape and are usually eager to help with this job. Once the flowers are in separate piles, gather up several stems into a bunch and bind their ends together with a rubber band. Hang the bundles upside down to dry in a dark, well-ventilated area, such as a warm attic. Drying times will vary depending on the type of flower, weather and temperature of the drying area. Plan on at least a week or two. When the petals and stems are dry to the touch, your children can begin their craft projects.

The following is a short list of annual dried flowers that are easy to grow and come in a variety of shapes, sizes and colors.

Common name: Globe Amaranth
Scientific name: *Gomphrena globosa*
Color: pink, purple, white, orange
Height: 1'–1½'
Part used: flower
When to harvest: Cut the flowers when they are fully open.

Common name: Winged Everlasting
Scientific name: *Ammobium alatum*
Color: white
Height: 2'
Part used: flower
When to harvest: Cut the flowers just before their yellow centers begin to show. They will open further as they dry, exposing the centers.

Common name: Strawflowers
Scientific name: *Helichrysum bracteatum*
Color: yellow, white, orange, red, pink, salmon
Height: 3'
Part used: flower
When to harvest: Strawflowers continue to open as they dry, so pick them when only one or two rows of petals have opened.

Common name: Love-in-a-mist
Scientific name: *Nigella damascena*
Color: green
Height: 1'–1½'
Part used: seed pod
When to harvest: Cut the pods when they have fully developed.

Common name: Larkspur
Scientific name: *Delphinium consolida*
Color: white, pink, purple
Height: 3'
Part used: flower
When to harvest: Cut when the flowers at the bottom of the flower spike are fully open but there are still several green buds at the top of the spike.

Common name: Statice
Scientific name: *Limonium sinuatum*
Color: white, purple, pink, blue, yellow, peach
Height: 1'–1½'
Part used: flower
When to harvest: Cut the flowers when they are in full bloom.

Potpourri

Potpourri is a colorful mixture of dried botanicals, such as flower heads, petals, leaves and seed pods. These ingredients, perfumed with fragrant oils, can be displayed in baskets and bowls or placed in fabric sachet bags to scent rooms, closets and drawers. Potpourri will be enjoyed by everyone in the family, yet is so simple to make that even young children can participate in this fun project.

Ingredients for making potpourri (from left to right): larkspur, globe amaranth, winged everlasting, love-in-a-mist, a bowl of potpourri made from the surrounding ingredients, and strawflowers

MATERIALS LIST

assorted flowers, leaves, and botanicals suitable for drying (such as dried flowers, rose petals, citrus peel, small pine cones, leaves, etc.)

decorative container(s)

essential oil

eyedropper

large glass or ceramic bowl

spoon

rubber bands

drying rack (optional)

Creating Potpourri

Two methods can be used to dry the floral ingredients for your potpourri. The first method is similar to the harvesting techniques given on the previous page. Cut the flower stems long and bind small bunches together with rubber bands. Hang them in a dark area to dry. Once the stems and flowers are crisp, simply pluck the flower heads from the stems. If you want to add ingredients to your potpourri that are not easily hung, such as orange and lemon peel, rose petals or leaves, you will need a drying rack. The rack need not be fancy; a simple window screen or a piece of muslin stretched and tacked across a wooden frame will do nicely. Scatter the ingredients across the screen in a single layer and place the rack in a dark area with good air circulation to dry.

Once your ingredients are dry, assemble them, keeping the colors and plant varieties separate. In a large glass or ceramic bowl, let your children mix the different flower colors together. This mixture will have very little scent, so add a drop or two of an essential oil for fragrance (essential oils are available at craft stores and come in a variety of scents). Parental assistance may be necessary to help children apply just a small amount with an eyedropper. Gently turn the potpourri with a spoon to mix the ingredients. Fill open baskets and bowls with their colorful batch of fragrant potpourri. This is a wonderful project for holiday time; homemade gifts are always appreciated, especially when they are made by children.

Pressed-Flower Notebook

This little notebook can be used as a diary, a sketchbook or a note keeper. Every other page is decorated with a

Keep notes and summer memories tucked away in this little pressed-flower notebook

small arrangement of pressed flowers, leaving plenty of room for notes and doodles. The loose-leaf rings make it easy to add extra pages. Your children will enjoy making, using and giving these special little books as gifts.

MATERIALS LIST

20 4" × 6" index cards (unlined)

2 4" × 6" sheets of colored construction paper or card stock

2 ¾" loose-leaf rings

assortment of pressed flowers

craft glue

facial tissues

thick telephone book

felt-tip pen

Creating a Pressed-Flower Notebook

The pressed-flower notebook begins with your children going out to the garden to collect a variety of flowers, leaves and grasses. Pansies, buttercups, lobelia, and larkspur press easily. Flowers wilt quickly, so encourage your children to pick only a few at a time.

Use a thick telephone book as a flower press. Open the book to the back pages and place a single tissue across the page. Then, put the flowers, leaves and grasses on the tissue, face down. Carefully drape a second tissue over the flowers, making sure the petals and leaves are not folded or touching one another. Grasp a ¼-inch-thick section of phone book pages and turn them on top of the second tissue. If you have more flowers to press continue on in the same manner: lay down the tissues and flowers and place a ¼-inch

section of pages between the layers. Leave the flowers undisturbed for about 2 weeks.

Once the flowers are dry, your children can assemble their notebooks. Start by punching two holes in all the index cards and colored cover sheets along their left-hand edge. Next, cut a window in the front cover to expose the first page of the book. A rectangle window was used on the book pictured; however, your children might choose a circle, a star or a heart shape. As a finishing touch, use a felt-tip pen to draw a borderline around the cut-out window.

To create the pressed-flower arrangement for the window, place the front cover over the first white page and lightly trace around the window cutout with a pencil. Remove the cover and let your children arrange the pressed flowers within the borders of the traced line. Once they like their design, the flowers can be glued in place. To keep the cover from rubbing against the floral picture, glue the cover to the first page, centering the cutout over the pencil line.

Stack the white cards between the two cover sheets and attach the loose-leaf rings. As your children press more flowers throughout the summer, they can add them to the interior pages in the same manner. They can also use their newly learned skills with pressed flowers to make greeting cards, wall plaques and bookmarks.

Dried-Flower Necklace and Head Wreath

From a small bed of everlastings, create fancy floral necklaces and head wreaths fresh from the garden. Your children will enjoy making and wearing these colorful decorations. On sunny summer days, this project can be done right in the garden, where the materials are close at hand.

Stringing dried-flower head wreaths and necklaces on a sunny summer day

A closer look at the finished products

MATERIALS LIST

fresh flower heads and seed pods suitable for drying (such as strawflowers, winged everlasting, globe amaranth, love-in-a-mist)

darning needle (necklace)

60" embroidery floss (necklace)

20" 17-gauge wire (head wreath)

6½ yards of ribbon (head wreath)

needlenose pliers (head wreath)

Creating a Dried-Flower Necklace and Head Wreath

Start by collecting a variety of fresh flowers and seed heads that are suitable for drying. Have your children pluck the heads off so that very little stem remains. To make a necklace, thread a darning needle with a long piece of embroidery floss. Double the thread and knot the ends. With close supervision, help your children string each flower onto the needle like a bead. Some of the flower centers are very firm, so you may need to push the needle through, and then let your children pull the flowers down the string. However, some flowers, like love-in-a-mist pods, are very easy for a child to string. Begin the necklace by pushing the first flower down the thread leaving a 2-inch tail at the end. Add more flowers until the necklace is your desired length. Cut the needle off and tie the two ends of the necklace together.

The head wreaths are made in much the same way. Start by gently curving the 20-inch piece of wire into a half circle. With needle-nose pliers, bend the tip of one end back onto itself, creating a small loop. Using the other end like a needle, your children can push the flowers onto the wire and slide them down to the looped end. Once the wire is completely strung with flowers, make a loop on the other end. Tie long streamer ribbons to each loop. Place the wreath on your child's head and tie the streamers together at the back in a big bow.

These necklaces and head wreaths can be worn immediately, even while they are fresh. Within a few days, the flowers will be dry and your children can enjoy them for weeks to come.

SUNFLOWERS

Children and sunflowers flourish in summertime gardens

Like pumpkins, sunflowers are wonderful plants to grow if you are introducing children to gardening. The large seeds are easy to handle and germinate quickly. Growing a giant flower that stands 6–12 feet tall is a rewarding experience for both children and adults.

Sunflowers come in a variety of colors and heights and all flourish in rich garden soil that receives regular watering. In spring, sow the seeds directly in the ground once all danger of frost has past. Depending on their size at maturity, thin the plants so they stand 12–36 inches apart.

For children, each stage in a sunflower's growth can be a learning experience. This giant flower will provide fun projects throughout the year, from planting seeds in early spring to sharing the harvest of seeds with birds in late winter.

Edible Flower Petals

By midsummer, the seeds your children planted in spring have developed into tall plants with large, nodding yellow flowers. The bright petals are edible and can be used to decorate salads, main dishes and desserts (see warnings, tips and recipes for edible flowers on pages 148–150). Children harvesting petals from the tallest sunflowers may need to be hoisted in the air to reach the large heads!

Harvesting Sunflower Seeds

By late summer, the flowers become pendulous from the weight of their seeds. They can now be harvested and turned into nutritious snacks for both humans and birds. Quite often, birds will start their snacking before your children have had their chance. Covering the heads with cheesecloth until the seeds are fully developed can discourage these early opportunists.

No matter what their size, sunflowers are bold, bright and beautiful

Once the heads have matured, cut the stems 1 foot below the heads using pruning shears and hang them in a warm, airy location. When the heads are completely dry, the seeds are easily coaxed from the seed head. Your children can crack open the shells and eat the seeds raw or, with supervision, lightly roast them on a cookie sheet in the oven.

To share your harvest with birds during the cold winter months, simply hang the dried seed heads from tree branches. After carefully observing these new objects, the birds will soon be flocking to the nutritious free meal.

Too tall to harvest!

Metric Equivalency Chart

Inches to Centimeters

inches	cm	inches	cm	inches	cm
⅛	0.3	9	22.9	30	76.2
¼	0.6	10	25.4	31	78.7
⅜	1.0	11	27.9	32	81.3
½	1.3	12	30.5	33	83.8
⅝	1.6	13	33.0	34	86.4
¾	1.9	14	35.6	35	88.9
⅞	2.2	15	38.1	36	91.4
1	2.5	16	40.6	37	94.0
1¼	3.2	17	43.2	38	96.5
1½	3.8	18	45.7	39	99.1
1¾	4.4	19	48.3	40	101.6
2	5.1	20	50.8	41	104.1
2½	6.4	21	53.3	42	106.7
3	8.9	22	55.9	43	109.2
3½	8.9	23	58.4	44	111.8
4	10.2	34	61.0	45	114.3
4½	11.4	25	63.5	46	116.8
5	12.7	26	66.0	47	119.4
6	15.2	27	68.6	48	121.9
7	17.8	28	71.1	49	124.5
8	20.3	29	73.7	50	127.0

Index

About the Authors

MICHAEL GERTLEY began his career in freelance photography at the age of sixteen, as a "stringer" for local newspapers. For over twenty-five years he has explored most areas of photography, including news, portrait and commercial work. However, his first love has always been photographing nature, with an emphasis on plants.

JAN GERTLEY has a college background in art and botany. For years she worked as a freelance designer, creating large props and whimsical window displays for retail stores. After marrying Michael in 1987, she started a dried-flower growing business. They moved to a rural community in western Washington and grew flowers commercially for eight years before turning their focus to writing.

The couple now collaborate on writing, photographing and illustrating magazine articles and books on garden-related topics.